Modern Madness

A Wild Schizoanalysis of Mental Distress in the Spaces of Modernity

Ed Lord

This book is dedicated to Sarah Lord and to the memory of John Lord. I am more grateful to both than words could adequately express.

I would also like to acknowledge with gratitude Theo Stickley, for showing me what a nurse could be, and Marcus Doel, for introducing me to critical spatial theory.

Winter Oak Press, Sussex, England, 2016

winteroak.org.uk

ISBN: 978-0-9576566-7-3

CONTENTS

INTRODUCTION

"To assert that we can be
whole/enlightened/healed within the present
madness amounts to endorsing the madness"
(John Zerzan)[1]

It often seems that Psychiatry is an easy target. As a discipline it has been rocked by criticism from within and without since its inception and especially so since the 1960's. As Pilgrim states "Psychiatric diagnosis has weathered nearly a century of criticism. It is now in a contradictory position"[2]. This contradiction is the widespread critique of psychiatry as a coercive pseudoscience that medicalises distress alongside its still accepted legitimacy by many groups and its official status within healthcare and legal systems. This situation is analogous to a contradiction of modernity; its widespread criticism but continued proliferation. This analogy works because "psychiatry is a quintessentially modernist project. Psychiatry and modernism arose from a very similar mind-set. Indeed, one is not understandable without the other"[3].

In this book I wish to explore this contradiction further and to identify deviations and rebellions from the modernist schema that could prove effective in the search for a new paradigm of understanding distress. I will explore some concepts of modernity, including the "Solid" and "Liquid" metaphors of Zygmunt Bauman[4], the 'domesticated alienation' of John Zerzan[5] and other theorists of Post-modernity, anti-modernity and Critical Theory. This will establish in what ways Psychiatry can be seen as an artefact of modernity and, if this is indeed the case, what is wrong with modernity as a paradigm. The early section of this investigation will also explore the already extant criticism of psychiatry, taking in contestations to the methodologies and definitions of mental disorder, the so called anti-psychiatry of thinkers such as Thomas Szatz and RD Laing, service user/survivor activism and the recent emergence of a literature coalescing under the banner of post-psychiatry. Wider criticism of institutions, knowledge and power such as those of Ivan Illich and Michel Foucault have relevance to this debate and will also be drawn upon.

A key premise of this work is that there is a profound dis-ease at the heart of modernity. Psychiatry is interesting in this regard in that it is both culpable in the problem as an artefact of that modernity whilst also being a 'warning beacon' identifying anxiety and distress in the population. There will be those who disagree with this premise, arguing that things are generally getting better and in this case why attempt to fix that which isn't broken. To explore this issue it is helpful to identify what we are referring to with the term 'modernity'. In the one sense modernity can be seen as a particular period in time emerging after the European Enlightenment[6]. Felix Guattari described Modernity as the shift from "the age of European Christianity" to "the age of the capitalistic deterritorialization of knowledges and techniques"[7]. The Enlightenment is associated with the coming to pre-eminence of the scientific world-view, post-monarchy ways of organising political systems and the dominance of capital within and beyond economic spheres. Philosophers associated with the emergence of modernity include Descartes, Kant, Bentham and Bacon. Modernity can be seen as having two strands, a cultural project and a social project: the project of the Enlightenment as the cultural strand and the encapsulation of a particular civilisational model in the European/Western process of societal modernisation as the social strand[8]. The Enlightenment, building on the Renaissance and Reformation, was a shift away from the medieval and early-modern world-view of tradition, myth, religion and rule by absolute monarchy. This included raising scientific methodologies as the preferred way to explain all manner of phenomena. Such methodologies included inductivism, in which observations of a particular case are used to generate theories that can predict future incidences/behaviours. This, and other scientific methodologies, tends to rely on the assumption that objective truths can be discovered by the rational examination of phenomena reduced to their constituent parts. This assumption is known as reductionism. These Enlightenment methods were also seen as applying to social organization, including identifying the autonomy of the individual subject as a rational actor (the 'metaphysics of the subject') and seeing society as able to manipulate non-human entities to 'create' an 'ideal' space.

The age of Enlightenment and emergence of modernity coincided with the exploration and colonisation of continents beyond Europe. This is the social project of modernity that exported European/Western ways of living and governing at the same time these new rationalities were being established at home. It is interesting in this regard that although Celtic monks are believed to have sailed as far as North America in the period commonly known as the 'dark ages' (the legendary "Voyage of St Brendan") the continent was not appropriated and exploited until maritime expeditions in the centuries leading up to the Enlightenment. The appropriation and exploitation required the technology, methodology, ideology and other factors tied up with the cultural and social project of emerging Modernity.

Modernity is also associated with the Industrial Revolution[9], seen by some as commencing in around 1710 and reaching its zenith between 1840 and 1880. This was a period characterised by an increasing pace of technological development, rapid urbanisation and a dramatic upswing in the rate of population growth. The 1710 date for commencement is somewhat arbitrary, stemming from the specific use of coke in a blast furnace by Abraham Darby, and the industrial revolution is arguably more accurately seen as a continuation of Enlightenment scientific thought.

All of these definitions of Modernity are an oversimplification of the issue however. The way I want to characterise Modernity is as an affect on everyday lived experience. An example of this is the description by Jay Griffiths of the changing conception of time as "wet and round time" and "dry and linear time" and how this is connected to social organisation, interpersonal relationships and the championing of particular technologies, in this case the clock[10]. Paul Virilio has also taken 'time' as a focus for exploring the everyday experience of modernity, using the term "Dromosphere" to describe the changing relations of space and time being lost in a compulsive speed acceleration. He talks of a "grey ecology" as a "pollution of distances" or a "pollution of life-size"[11] that should be as concerning as pollution of 'green' ecology. To approach modernity in this way is not to analyse cities, for example, as just another space, but to see the totality and wider implications of their very existence. Here we begin to unpeel the dark side of our 'taken for granted' epoch and in this sense "the tragic chorus is the city itself"[12]. To continue in this examination of negative 'affects' we see loss of foundations and a chimera of autonomy collapsing into fragmentation as common impacts associated with modernity. The experience of this is expressed by Bauman as a paradox:

"The greater our individual freedom, the less it is relevant to the world in which we practice it. The more tolerant the world becomes of the choices we make, the less the game, our playing it, and the way we play it are open to our choice. No longer does the world appear amenable to kneading and moulding; instead, it seems to tower above us – heavy, thick and inert, opaque, impenetrable and impregnable, stubborn and insensitive to any of our intentions, resistant to our attempts to render it more hospitable to human co-existence" (Zygmunt Bauman)[13].

This paradox gets to the heart of the failure of the Enlightenment. Despite claims that 'rationality' is a liberation from superstition, it becomes instead a "disenchantment of the world" (in the words of Max Weber), a reduction of everyday possibility. The Enlightenment has turned out to be "as totalitarian as any system"(Adorno and Horkheimer)[14] and we find that "the fully enlightened earth radiates disaster triumphant"[15]. Sigmund Freud[16] joins Theodor Adorno and Max Horkheimer in suggesting that repression becomes a daily necessity just to exist and function in this paradigm. In this personal repression and 'radiant disaster' everyday life has been reduced and debased by the instrumental rationality[17] of a "techno-scientific imagination [that] has structured itself for some six hundred years around the concept of disappearance – of the inexorable enactment of a stripping down of the world, of the substance of the living world" (Paul Virilio)[18].

One of the central tenets of the modernist world-view is a faith in 'progress'. This is the belief that time is on a linear trajectory and that 'development' is taking humanity to a progressively improved mode of living[19]. One frequently finds an unquestioned adherence to this myth and it can often be supported only by a narrow quantitative appraisal of one particular field of knowledge to the exclusion of wider factors or, to use the language of economics, 'externalities'.

The experience of space and place can again use affect to imply that modernity is a flawed project. This includes the loss of a feeling of familiarity and ease in places known and experienced at different stages in the lifespan[20] or the violence inherent in the suppression of the natural, sensory and sensual to establish abstract space[21]. Some of the large global scale problems that seem beyond the systems of conventional discourse to solve are another sign of the failure of modernity. This includes anthropogenic climate change[22] and increasing inequality and oppressive modes of commodity production accompanying the globalization of neo-liberal economic ideology[23].

The analysis of space can bring the discussion back to psychiatry. The space of psychiatric treatment has changed over the last 20-30 years, with the closure of large institutions with many inpatient beds and the increase of 'community care'. This pattern can be linked to a shift within modernity characterised by some as post-modernity[24], by others as high-modernity[25] and still others as light capitalism or liquid modernity[26]. Bauman discusses at length the end of a belief in progress that drove early modernism and the hubris of its 'captains of industry' and colonial administrations[27]. Despite this loss of belief in progress, Bauman suggests the logic of progress still drives society, it is just that upon entering the cockpit the passenger will find it empty and the plane flying automatically to an unknown and undisclosed destination. Virilio announces the coming of an 'instantaneity' that signals the end of a 'life size' relationship between time and space[28]. He describes this as the advent of the 'communications revolution' to replace the 'transportation revolution' of earlier modernity. Bauman phrases the shift as from the 'wetware' of the pre-modern, via the 'hardware' of the modern (such as the large 'Fordist' factory) to the 'software' of the post/late/liquid modern.

For my exploration of the state of psychiatry these characterisations of change will be drawn upon. The twilight of the large asylum can be easily pictured in Hardt's image of the walls of the institutions breaking down[29]. But this breaking down is not an emancipation but just the replacing of Foucault's disciplinary society[30] by Deleuze's "societies of Control"[31]. Despite widespread anecdotes of the bad old days of the asylum it seems more accurately that this is a myth of progress, as Vetter puts it:

> "neo-panopticism is defined by an ever expanding field of observational measures at the very moment that the institutional regimentation of bodies is coming to an end" (Grant Vetter)[32]

With this insight as the background along with the ongoing ineffectiveness of psychiatry to provide resolution to distress[33] and the premise that a profound dis-ease exists within the experience of modernity a radical 'line of flight'[34] will be sought. This book will not take the presence of modernity as a given, but will challenge this setting (or hosting) of psychiatry as a way to de-territorialise psychiatry, prevent its immediate re-territorialising as a neo-panoptic technique and to explore potential radical subversions to its hegemony over the classification and remedy of distress.

The radical practice devised by Deleuze and Guattari known as Schizoanalysis[35] will be used as an analytical tool to criticise what is extant whilst resisting a disabling premature re-territorialisation. Schizoanalysis, in this context, will act as "an anti-rule rule, [and] will enforce a constant calling into question" (Felix Guattari)[36].

In this Schizoanalysis there is a need to counter the authority given to expert systems within modernity along with the tendency of disembedding time from space to create malleable subdivided and striated 'empty' dimensions[37]. To this end specific and richly contextual cases will be examined in depth. The main cases selected for this illustrative purpose are the Zapatista movement in southern Mexico, the 'Idle No More' activities focused upon First Nations communities in North America and the art and literary project known as 'The Dark Mountain Project' in the United Kingdom. It may seem surprising that none of these cases is focused specifically upon mental health issues, but this is deliberately done in order to break down the functional specialisation that has so far prevented the escape of lines of flight from the codified disciplinary boundaries of psychiatry. Through this it is hoped to ventilate knowledge as "connaissance", a critique of what exists, beyond and through the boundaries imposed by "savoir" knowledge that colludes with power (Henri Lefebvre)[38].

SITUATING MENTAL DISTRESS AND MODERNITY

FELIX GUATTARI AND SCHIZOANALYSIS

The language of analysis selected for this investigation may make little sense to the uninitiated and is likely to lead to misunderstanding if a grounding and rationale is not provided. The terms of reference owe much to the work of Gilles Deleuze and Felix Guattari. Most obviously I am drawing upon their shared works known as 'Capitalism and Schizophrenia', published in two parts, 'Anti-Oedipus'[39] and 'A Thousand Plateaus'[40]. The material of my analysis is not exclusively from these editions, however, and their considerable further solo and joint published literature will also be drawn upon. Particularly useful to the methodology used in my analysis will be their idea of 'Schizoanalysis' and the development of this concept by Guattari right up to his death in 1992. Their collaboration marked the synthesis of two diverse figures: Deleuze, the philosopher within the academic institution, and Guattari, the political activist and professional psychotherapist. According to Dosse they had a friendship and intellectual affinity which managed to never become fusional and their writing became more than the sum of two individuals[41].

Their thinking and creation of concepts was very much a product of the theoretical vacuum highlighted by the large student and worker uprisings of 1968, in Paris and elsewhere around the world. In this vein Anti-Oedipus has been described as a May '68 book[42]. Anti-Oedipus, as an oversimplification, could be described as the critique of what is extant, the frustrating impasse that had been reached, while A Thousand Plateaus, as the second part, has quite a different structure and provides a conceptual tool kit to envisage something different. The core argument of the two books centres around 'desire' and particularly a 'revolution of desire'. Deleuze and Guattari put this idea forth as a contradiction and opposition to the psychoanalytic theory of Freud and Lacan of the unconscious being stuck within the narrative of the Oedipal cycle. They suggest that the unconscious instead functions as a machine of 'production' and this production they characterise as 'desire'. Psychoanalysis therefore becomes a tool of the dominant order, which they "reproach [...] for having stifled this order of production [of desire], for having shunted it into representation"[43].

At this stage it should be pointed out that neither 'Capitalism and Schizophrenia' nor 'Schizoanalysis' is exclusively about mental health, ill-health, psychotherapy or psychiatry. The analysis they are proposing crosses disciplinary boundaries and is as critical of political structure and institutions, aesthetics, linguistics, semiotics, media, physical sciences and a whole host of other domains as it is of 'psy' specialities. They are focused on the creation and constitution of subjectivity and how dominant discourses are framed by structural and transcendental narratives. Their use of the term 'schizophrenic' as a paragon of revolutionary desire creation seems initially confusing to those more familiar with schizophrenia as a clinical entity, but their use is set against the idea of the 'neurotic' constitution of statist and rigid rule-bound psychoanalytic subjectivity. It indicates a crossing of socially enforced 'norms' or boundaries to a way of thinking that is in 'flux'[44] and will not neurotically repress 'lines of flight' before they can creatively connect with different and/or heterogeneous domains. The emphasis in

Deleuze and Guattari's work on the 'event', the 'singularity' and 'becoming' over fixity and rigidity cannot be overstated, they identify subjectivity as being situated and constituted by its context, in this analysis, the capitalist milieu. In situating their analysis in its context they can begin to answer the problematic: why does it seem we desire our servitude as if it were our salvation? (having borrowed this question from Spinoza)[45]. This is also my problematic in conducting a schizoanalysis of distress and "the outcome may be a de-territorialization [....], out of which is produced a nomadic subject, a point of intensity which enables becoming, or to put it otherwise, enables resistance, enables the realization that things could be different"[46].

This nomadic subject using nomadic thought is not casting away from the world, however, in some irrelevant quest of abstraction. To think in a nomadic way is to find a becoming that can eliminate "all forms of organization, signification, and subjectification standing between our desires and our perceptions so that they correlate precisely, thus enabling us to launch forth from home on the thread of a tune, to improvise with the world, and ultimately to meld with it" (Eugene Holland)[47]. In this way there is no divide between the unconscious, the conscious and the outside world, the critique can oscillate between the individual and the social, without ignoring either domain or falling into reductive binary thinking.

To begin to state a case for the use of novel concepts and new terminology, such as 'deterritorialisation' and 'nomad thought', we will return to my comments in the introduction about certain problems being intractable and beyond the scope of conventional/dominant discourse. Guattari attends to this point in an interview conducted in 1980 for the journal 'Liberation'[48]. He is challenged as to whether the difficulty posed by the "extremely abstract nature of the language" is an "elitist gesture" or is necessitated by the object of the research[49]. His response is to champion the use of minor language as a tool "opening up a new set of questions". This is an attempt to express the ineffable[50], to drop pretensions to a universal language or philosophy and to identify attempts to do so as replicating/re-enforcing 'major' relations of domination. Becoming minor is a thematic that arises in numerous parts of Deleuzo-Guattarian thought, including minor-arts, minor-cinema[51], minor science[52] and minor literature/language[53].

Deleuze and Guattari discuss their concept of 'minor science' as akin to 'nomad science' in their chapter (or 'plateau') on Nomadology[54]. They present this as a contrast to 'royal' or 'state' science ('major' science). The nomad/minor science is concerned with "becoming and heterogeneity" or, in their terminology of space, a "smooth space" which is "occupied without being counted". The royal/state/major science is, conversely, concerned with "the stable, the eternal, the identical, the constant" or "striated space" which is "counted in order to be occupied"[55]. This conflict between the smooth nomad who thinks, organises and moves as a Rhizome and the striated state form which thinks and organises in an arboreal/hierarchical fashion, according to Deleuze and Guattari, is the essential distinction to grasp when searching for tools that can express desire. This thinking is both to do with actual physical presence in which Nomads exist in parts of the world and relate to territories in a particular way, and also a tool of philosophy to apply to a given problematic. This is how I intend to approach the subject of distress within the context of modernity, both as a physical problem within space and as a philosophical problematic. Deleuze and Guattari walk a fine line between the two, attempting to maintain a diverse and different heterogeneity, in the face of the dominant inclination to choose between one and the other as a binary either/or.

Guattari's work as an activist and within the radical psychiatric clinic called La Borde is instructive within this analysis. It must be emphasised, however, that this will not be to provide a blueprint of how mental health services/psychiatry should be structured differently. It would be to fall into the trap of arboreal thinking to impose a top-down universal system. That is frequently the way research is filtered down into practice and institutional policy, according to Holmes, Gestaldo and Perron, in this application the evidence based discourse becomes a 'micro-fascism' crowding out diversity and multiplicity of knowledge[56]. Guattari repeatedly states that La Borde is not his proposal for an "ideal model"[57]. Also La Borde cannot be transposed "to the whole of society, no single model being transposable in this way"[58]. It is more use as an example of responsiveness to local conditions, openness to singularisations, and of how to ensure that heterogeneous flux and flow can come together into particular assemblages. Just as the Rhizome grows in non-linear and unpredictable directions.

ANARCHIC SPACE

Having introduced Deleuze and Guattari's thought and how it will be applied in this investigation I will now introduce the idea of anarchist thought and space. The enforcement of a particular type of space is closely intertwined with the denial of varied/heterogeneous types of thought. Mick Smith[59] discusses the demand for a whole new (or very old) concept of ethics and approach to law implicit in environmental problems that are largely the result of modernity. This discussion is equally transferable to an analysis of mental distress and psychiatric care in the context of modernity[60]. Gonzalez suggests that "anarchic/ist spaces and places do not fit within the current hegemonic geographical structures and frameworks, that we call the mosaic-statist metageography"[61]. Equally the discussion of different paradigms of distress doesn't fit within the hegemonic structures, not just of bio-medical psychiatry, but of much social and psychological modelling of mental distress as well. What has been produced by the dialectics, legalities and institutions of modernity is preventative of thinking 'outside' of modernity. Just as "the geographical imaginary produced by mosaic-statist metageography renders other spatial realities unimaginable"[62]. An anarchist approach to space is necessary for an analysis of distress because so many spatial practices of modernity, such as bordering, are simply taken for granted and are not analysed sufficiently in an anti/post-modern light[63]. Anarchist practice is distinct from 'representative' political movements in that it is prefigurative, it builds the world it wants to see in the here and now, rather than waiting for external authority to act or to risk replicating the oppressive systems it opposes in the practice of struggle and process. A prefigurative approach to territorialisation is thus an approach that "opens up our spatial and political imaginations to radical alternatives"[64].

In his critique of the thought of Le Corbusier using Lefebvre's works, Mick Smith[65] argues that the elimination of difference is central to modernity's desire for its own 'clear site'. This creates the "social and natural vacuum of the 'non-place'"[66], which is not really a 'clear site', but an "extremely anti-social space"[67]. This supposed 'clear site' (of space and thought) is established and maintained with insidious and on-going violence[68]. It requires a frontier to demarcate that which is 'within' and legally acceptable and that which is 'outside' and can be demonised and repressed by force[69]. Law and property is also significant in that it gives the right to 'expel' that which is undesirable[70]. This violence is often not enacted but is operative by being continually implied[71]. Thus "moral conformity is ensured precisely by excluding those who are different, who refuse to comply with the roles set out for them"[72]. This dramatically reduces the ways in which we can relate to one another, making all interaction "individualism and instrumentality"[73] and naturalising this as the "ideological environment within which we exist"[74].

Thus to analyse the presence of debilitating distress within modernity I will seek an anarchist space, both physically actual and in the realm of concepts, beyond the 'frontier'[75]. In this way I will attempt to not collude with power or the hegemony of statist/modernist worldviews, whilst acknowledging that I personally am a product of this context[76]. The perspective of 'difference' will be brought to bear upon the 'repetition' of my context, or as Guy Debord puts it "wanderings that express not subordination to randomness but total insubordination to habitual influences"[77]. As Blomley points out "for the homeless person, the renter, the squatter, the indigenous person, or the trade unionist, the violence meted out by the state in defence of the right to expel is too often undeniable"[78]. It is my intention, by analysing the problematic as a nomad in anarchic space, to open up a new set of questions and to risk an expulsion by violence.

DOMESTICATION

Having introduced the thought of Deleuze and Guattari and then situated anarchic space as the opening of possibilities to ask forbidden questions, it is timely now to introduce the final ingredient to my analytic mix. This ingredient is the critique of modernity offered by John Zerzan. In his thinking Zerzan offers a profoundly non-statist way of approaching what he characterises as the alienation inherent to life within modernity. He frequently criticises thinkers who highlight problems with modernity but then collapse into a nihilistic acceptance of things as they are or propose reformist solutions that perpetuate the very problems they have identified. As he states in his essay "The Modern Anti-World", "Paradoxically, most contemporary works of social analysis provide grounds for an indictment of the modern world, yet fail to confront the consequences of the context they develop"[79].

For this refusal to avoid confronting the context, he presents a compelling and widely critiqued argument that takes steps towards building what Deleuze and Guattari could conceptualize as a "nomad war machine" in their Nomadology plateau[80]. Zerzan's philosophy sits within the tradition of counter-Enlightenment thought and he frequently refers to the critique developed by Frankfurt School theorists, especially Benjamin, Adorno, Horkheimer and Marcuse. He identifies daily life within high modernity as being a "reified existence [that] progressively disables whatever and whoever questions it"[81]. Borrowing from some of Freud's work[82] he catalogues the repression involved in every step 'forward' of a progress that has "atrophied our senses, [and] repressed unmediated experience"[83]. This repression hypothesis mirrors Levi-Strauss' suggestion that the 'civilised' reductionist scientific way of perceiving/studying the world mistrusts and downgrades the 'primitive' direct subjective experience provided by the senses[84]. Zerzan identifies reductionism as being a key barrier to envisaging, let alone participation in, a liberatory rhizomatic:

> "Systematic complexity fragments, colonizes, debases daily life. Division of labor, its motor, diminishes humanness in its very depths, dis-abling and pacifying us. This de-skilling specialization, which gives us the illusion of competence, is a key, enabling predicate of domestication." (John Zerzan)[85]

Zerzan's position critiquing division of labour and specialisation is strongly anti-technology, building upon the theories of technique and the nature of technological rationality put forward by

Jacques Ellul[86] and Lewis Mumford[87]. Technology can be identified as a utopian myth which in turn supports a world view that comes to epitomise the rationality of progress[88]. Thus Zerzan believes that the humanist/modernist anarchism of figures such as Bookchin and Chomsky, or the neo-Marxism/Stalinism of Zizek, miss the point in limiting their critiques to capitalism alone. Zerzan wants to problematize every institution of modernity and civilisation to expose the totality that colonises every moment of life.

His Anarcho-Primitivism is not to be confused, however, with the Romanticism of figures such as Rousseau (although he includes works of the romantics in his "Against Civilisation" anthology of 2005, along with heterogeneous other works). Whilst the romantics could be seen as half of a binary opposition between primitive and civilised[89], Zerzan's primitivism contains much more nuance and benefits from Indigenous voices being raised in protest movements and from the shifting scholarly/academic sands of de/post-colonial anthropology, archaeology and social theory. Mick Smith notes that the distinctiveness of ecological anarchism is that it "turns the idea of progress on its head in every sense, technological, social, political, and moral"[90]. The anarcho-primitivist stance has been criticised widely for its deployment of a 'mystical' worldview in place of a 'rational' one. This critique, however, misses the point in that anarcho-primitivism is not simply a neo-romanticism. Its seeming deployment of 'myths' could be regarded as a necessary foil to the no-less mythical belief in a 'rational progress'[91]. "If myths are expressive of the forms of life that constitute them then ecological anarchism at least has the merit of pointing out in no uncertain terms that these particular (modernist) myths have begun to wear a little thin given the realities of everyday life and the scale of environmental destruction" (Mick Smith)[92].

As noted above, domestication is a premise of this more nuanced critique of civilisation. Kay Anderson's[93] attempt to open up a critical geography of domestication raises some of the issues that Zerzan has theorized in depth since the 1980's. Domestication is the practice by which animals and plants are selected and protectively bred by humans and is fundamental to the emergence of agriculture during the Neolithic period 11,000 years ago. Anderson argues that despite a large scientific literature on domestication it has largely "escaped critical sociological attention from human scientists"[94].

Domestication has been identified by numerous authors, such as Jared Diamond and Steven Mithen, as more significant than industrialisation and capitalism[95] in creating the problems of modernity. As Mithen sums up in the epilogue of his epic history of the Mesolithic/Neolithic era:

> "A world of temporary campsites had been transformed into one with villages and towns, a world with mammoths had been transformed into one with domesticated sheep and cattle. The path towards the huge global disparities of wealth with which we live today had been set." (Steven Mithen)[96]

The process of plant and animal domestication and the changes to lifestyles thus brought about can be seen to have domesticated humans also. "Just as humans domesticate plants so do they themselves become domesticated within a political structure that will come to dominate them" (Michael Becker)[97]. Much like the violent inside and outside necessitated by property[98], domestication can be seen as a spatial practice, in establishing a 'domus' defended from the dangerous 'wild'[99]. This has interesting resonances in issues relating to gender roles and the 'essentialising' of feminine characteristics as residing in the domestic space[100] or as a 'wild' other in need of taming[101]. This essentialising of the feminine contributes to a gender binary (either/or) which sits alongside numerous simplistic oppositional binaries. Anderson's argument, along with that of Zerzan, is that a problematising of domestication is long overdue and can bring into view fresh insights on social and environmental problems and the 'everyday' of modernity.

Zerzan advocates the undermining of modernity by re-wilding, a concept that I will develop later. To combine a Guattarian Schizoanalysis with Zerzan's anarcho-primitivism is a novel concept and may initially appear to be an uncomfortable fit. The connections between the two thinkers are, however, compelling. Whilst Guattari was active in French communist circles during the 1950's and 1960's, Zerzan was being politicised by the vibrant counter culture emerging in San Francisco as he was studying at University in the Bay area. From this shared Leftist grounding they both experienced the profound questions raised by May '68 and, particularly for Zerzan, the anti-Vietnam War mobilisations. This led Guattari into the fertile partnership with Deleuze, their novel theorizing and on the ground activism. For Zerzan this led through radical labour union organising amongst social services staff and clients, a period of disillusionment, academic research posts and an emergence in the 1980's as one of the most distinctive contemporary anarchist thinkers. The closest resonance between the two is their commitment to radical publishing and media production pursued throughout their careers as activists.

THE CRITIQUE OF PSYCHIATRY

In this literature review, and in this investigation more widely, the existing critiques of psychiatry cannot be ignored. Indeed, given the long standing contestation of psychiatry, a strong case must be made to justify my argument as necessary, having utility and as distinct from what has been stated previously. I would like to suggest that there are three broad strands to the existing critique. Firstly there is a wider problematisation of medicine (and scientific knowledge itself) as a discipline. Secondly there is the criticism of psychiatry as a distinct specialism within medicine and whether it is appropriate to situate it within this profession. Finally there is the overt power/status of psychiatry within the legal systems of many nation states giving its practices authority to be enforced without consent. These are three distinct positions to approach a critique from, each can stand alone substantially, but it must also be acknowledged that they are interlinked. A simplistic separation of these three strands is possible in my analysis, as is a linear chronological account, and I readily identify the pitfalls of such an approach. I will revisit this issue towards the end of this section.

To take the first critique, that of medicine and scientific knowledge, is a vast undertaking. As something of an overview I will draw upon the work of Ivan Illich, Michel Foucault and Jacques Ellul to illustrate the contested nature of medicine and advanced healthcare systems. This is part of the wider "sociology of scientific knowledge" that has sought to challenge scientific disciplines' claim to produce neutral objective information[102]. The suggestion that scientific knowledge is socially constructed has ramifications for any research or practice that is claiming to produce a-historical universally applicable techniques. Medicine (broadly speaking) falls into this category, especially when one considers the promotion of clinical guidelines and 'evidence based practice/medicine/health sciences' (EBP, EBM or EBHS). Holmes likens this to Foucault's concept of a 'micro-fascism', the widely championed Cochrane review process acting as an enforcer of the established hierarchy, a single discourse of the extant paradigm[103];

> "we are currently witnessing the health sciences engaged in a strange process of eliminating some ways of knowing. EBHS becomes a 'regime of truth', as Foucault would say – a regimented and institutionalised version of 'truth' (Holmes, Murray, Perron and Rail)[104].

In addition to the use of Foucault to suggest that medicine privileges one discourse amongst many, it has been proposed that medicine has a dark side that has the opposite effect of promoting health. Illich's "Limits to Medicine"[105] was a landmark study that explored the active damage done by medical intervention, including iatrogenesis, and the production of "a morbid society that demands universal medicalization and a medical establishment that certifies universal morbidity"[106]. Since the 1970's this trend can be seen to have accelerated, especially with the growing dominance of pharmaceutical companies and the globalisation of 'western' models of health care. Everyday issues are becoming pathologised and reduced to technical bio-physiological problems to be 'treated', or as Conrad states "medical designations are increasingly defining what is normal, expected, and acceptable in life"[107].

Medicine can also be seen as a 'technique' in Ellul's theory of technological systems requiring mass society, standardisation and the framing of a particular 'milieu' within which to operate[108]. In this way, despite ostensibly benign intentions from most practitioners, medical systems become just another 'assembly line' amongst many other similar systems required for technology to function. In a post-traditional society, care has gone from the "sanctuary" to the "laboratory", "dispassionate skills" of treatment technologies are privileged over and divorced from caring in the daily activities of health care workers[109].

The implications for psychiatry are evident within these wider critiques of medicine and scientific knowledge. The strength of this strand lies in the ability to join up struggles across specialities. An example of this, using the same area of critique, from outside of psychiatry is the case of the medicalisation of child birth. Thus the micro-fascism of 'evidence based' obstetric practice is highlighted by the "Birth Without Violence" hypothesis of Leboyer[110], the feminist critique of medicalised child birth[111] and the 'other' represented by non-western practices.

The second strand of the extant critique is directly focused upon psychiatry itself, whether it is appropriate to be located within the discipline of medicine and the deficiencies of seeing human distress in this way. This critique can be demonstrated by an historical overview of the development of the discipline of medicine. It is important to note that psychiatry is a relatively recent addition to the domain of medicine, there being "no specialisation around the treatment of the mad until the early eighteenth century"[112]. This coincides with what Foucault characterised as the 'great confinement' of society's 'rejects and misfits'[113]. The breakdown of traditional wider family/community/feudal networks with new industrial working regimes during this period meant that it became increasingly difficult for families and communities to care for those who couldn't partake in the industrial working day. Some were 'confined' in workhouses or poorhouses, but the 'mad' or 'lunatics' presented a problem for the regimes of such institutions[114]. Thus specialist 'asylums' were established, initially on a financially lucrative private basis and following the British County Asylum Act of 1808 publicly funded. These institutions were not initially medically staffed and it has been argued that they presented the 'crucible' within which the discipline of psychiatry was forged. This would have been for various motives, sometimes paternalistic philanthropy, othertimes a belief in Enlightenment rationality and in many cases simply a desire to gain a monopoly and make financial profit from the provision of a service in demand (the growth of the 'emotion industry' discussed by Crossley[115]). Whatever the motives, "the history of professional psychiatry begins with the separation of the mentally ill into institutions" (Clarke)[116]. This birth amongst contingency and opportunity creates the basis for a critique of the discipline's legitimacy.

Beyond this historical analysis of its origins, psychiatry has been critiqued as a part of medicine for its disease concepts, diagnostic categories and prescribed treatments. Since the early attempts to classify mental illness according to a bio-medical model by figures such as Emil Kraepelin (eg, Schizophrenia/Dementia praecox discussed by Williams[117]), writing in the 1870's-1890's, numerous diagnostic manuals have been published. The key issue of contention here is that symptoms are listed for which no 'test' exists. "DSM criteria.... are not, in fact, complaints about bodily functioning (pain, nausea and so on). They are examples of beliefs, experiences and behaviours" (Johnstone)[118] (DSM stands for 'Diagnostic and Statistical Manual') and the assessment of such symptoms is based upon judgements that are philosophically, culturally and contextually situated in the value system of the diagnosing clinician[119]. As discussed earlier (when introducing Enlightenment thought) scientific inquiry is claimed to have an objectively verifiable process, the medical model is just such a science. Setting aside for a moment criticisms of the scientific process and objectivity, psychiatry fails to produce a classification system in the same fashion as most physical disease/illness processes.

"A moment's thought will demonstrate the far reaching implications for psychiatry as it is currently practised, including the use of medical language (symptom, illness, patient, treatment, remission, prognosis, etc); the typical settings (hospitals, wards, clinics); the medical training of key professionals (nurses and doctors); and the basic interventions (medication, ECT). All of these taken-for-granted aspects of psychiatry would be challenged by a threat to its diagnostic system and hence to its current status as a branch of medical science" (Lucy Johnstone)[120].

The third strand of critique takes us into

another angle with which to problematize the practice and institution of psychiatry. This is its status within healthcare and legal systems in many countries. The medical model of healthcare is funded publicly and by various other means in much of the Western world and in this sense has something of a hegemonic status. To some extent, however, people are able to choose not to receive the assessments, investigations, interventions and treatments offered or available. Psychiatry stands out from this in that there is routine legal provision in many countries for people to be detained against their will, assessed by psychiatric professionals, and for interventions and treatments to be administered coercively and by overt force. This third critique stands alone but is also given increased veracity if one considers the contested nature of psychiatric definitions, diagnosis and treatment discussed above.

This area of critique has been explored extensively by Thomas Szasz in his numerous written works and his clinical practice as a psychiatrist was on the basis that clients came to him voluntarily and on a privately funded basis[121]. "Szasz's position on coercive psychiatry... poses a challenge, especially for those in the 'mental health field',... who invariably become the 'psychiatric enforcers', willingly or otherwise" (Buchanan-Barker and Barker)[122]. The factor of legally enforcing admission and treatment is a constant stumbling block for those in mental health professions attempting to argue for or develop a person-centred anti-oppressive 'helping' practice[123].

Having summarised some key critical positions already extant in this debate using three specific domains I will now present the critique of psychiatry through some social movements that emerged in the latter half of the 20th Century. Although, as already noted, psychiatry has been a field of contention from its very beginnings, certain movements stand out. Three will be discussed here, anti-psychiatry, service-user activism and critical/post-psychiatry. Anti-psychiatry is the broad term that has become attached to numerous radical authors and practitioners during the 1960's-70's. The most well know members of this movement were Laing, Cooper and Szasz. Laing and Cooper in the UK were close associates and their radical critique is associated with an existential and left wing ethos, Szasz is a US based psychiatrist and his radical critique is generally viewed as libertarian right wing. Laing became something of a cult figure during the 1960's and his most famous book "The Divided Self" had a readership far beyond the 'psy' professions[124]. Crossley puts the emergence of this radical critique and its difference from previous protests within psychiatry down to a three step combination of factors. These three were firstly, rejection of Laing's ideas within mainstream psychiatric circles, secondly, the emergence of 'the new left' with a strong interest in radical/critical publishing and finally the wider counter-culture that provided a receptive audience[125].

The anti-psychiatric movement is significant in that it came from within the profession but, for reasons stated above, resonated within the wider culture and thus represented a significant threat to the status and hegemony of medical psychiatry. The practical side of the movement in terms of the establishment of the therapeutic community known as 'Kingsley Hall' in London and the politicised orientations of organisations such as the Philadelphia Association was relatively short lived. This is taken by some as representing the failure of the movement, but the fact remains that a critical dialogue was opened and a critique was presented and widely disseminated. Whereas Laing and Cooper pursued less overtly public/popular interests from the mid 1970's and both died in the 1980's, Szasz continues publishing to this day and is unwavering in his refusal to concede to psychiatric 'quackery' and coercion[126]. His political views are very much in tune with the neo-liberal right and thus he has found an on-going niche within which to publish and practise[127]. In conclusion commonalities can be found which resonate with the sociological critiques from outside psychiatry, such as those of Foucault and Goffman. As an example of this: "in spite of the differences between Szasz and the anti-psychiatrists, one concern they share is a distaste for psychiatric coercion and state control of mental health services." (Coppock and Hopton)[128].

Anti-psychiatry is now largely seen as a historical movement and the radical proposals of figures such as Laing and Cooper are mostly forgotten in professional circles. Since the 1980's the look of psychiatric services has changed significantly, most obviously in the swift downsizing and closure of large hospitals and the initiation of community based services. In many Western countries, despite rhetoric of 'evidence based care', this has been mostly driven by neo-liberal small state ideology, in terms of scaling back public provision. Another aspect of this has been the construction of an individualistic consumer mentality, initially in consumer goods, but soon spilling over into service provision, including health care. It is fair to conclude that this mentality on top of the ground work initiated by the anti-psychiatry movement has led to the idea in psychiatry of 'service user involvement'. I do not doubt that the need to listen to the voices of those on the receiving end of psychiatric intervention is long overdue. Bearing this in mind, however, I have reservations about service user involvement, largely on the grounds that its deployment tends to leave the fundamental assumptions of psychiatry untouched. As an example of this, the use of legislation to detain and enforce treatment remains in place and is widely used. This is rarely overturned despite numerous 'checks and balances' such as (in the UK) the right to appeal a Mental Health Act detention and the right to advocacy. Another example is that the choice of medication to be prescribed will always be discussed with a patient, but very rarely will supported withdrawal from psychiatric medication be offered. It seems that in modern psychiatry we have created an echo chamber that has the glossy surface impression of involvement and choice but in practice and outcome is only marginally different from the psychiatry of 40 years ago.

This is why my wild schizoanalysis is necessary and needed. By criticising service user involvement I am not disparaging the need for multiple voices to be brought to bear on this issue. I am saying that the current excuse for involvement is little more than papering over the cracks in a stale ideology. I could liken this to the environmental movement, which saw radical groups such as 'Greenpeace' emerge in the 1960's and 1970's. In a similar fashion these radical proposals have been captured by consumer ideology, reified into NGOs and now too often 'greenwash' over the cracks in modernity. As with psychiatry, this leaves fundamental questions not only unanswered, but not even being asked. My investigation and suggestion of a new/novel methodology in wild schizoanalysis is thus justified. I am not so arrogant as to suggest I have transcended these existing critiques of psychiatry. I owe a debt to them all and I am building (or tearing down!?) upon their foundations. Particularly close to my research is the recent emergence of a literature under the title 'Post-psychiatry'[129]. This is a philosophical trend drawing upon the insights of the service user movement and post-structuralism to suggest that psychiatry is not and should not ever be a homogeneous single narrative. This is an inspiration, along with 'Mad Pride', the Critical Psychiatry Network, the Critical Mental Health Nurses Network and numerous other rebels, who comfort me that I am not alone in my questioning and frustration. My investigation will acknowledge and draw upon the tri-partite critique described above as well as anti-psychiatry, post-psychiatry and service user activism. I am, however, distinctive in explicitly challenging modernity as a context and will not hesitate to 'call out' these existing critical positions for the instances when they 'paper over the cracks' or fall short by 'greenwashing'.

A METHODOLOGICAL INSURRECTION

EVERYDAY METHODOLOGIES OF IMMANENCE AND AFFECT

"Good research requires understanding how method is embedded in methodology in real life applications" (Davies, Hoggart and Lees)[130].

Thus I come now to address the methodology of my investigation of mental distress in the spaces of modernity. The undertaking here is a qualitative exercise orientated to the theoretical, in that I am claiming "to develop some theoretical insights by means of a critical review of a body of literature" (Silverman)[131]. In undertaking this investigation I am not aiming to create an objective evidence base upon which policy can be formed or to elaborate a closely refined 'truth' with which to win a dialectical argument. To claim to do this would be to, firstly, participate in a disciplinary and reductive micro-fascist evidence-based discourse. Secondly this would fall into the binary trap of seeing my conclusion as half of a dialectical argument with which to beat down the 'opposite' position. Finally, it would be to over-estimate the scale and scope of what it is possible to achieve with the context, time and resources available to the research project being undertaken. In this sense the methodology is the research, to echo and appropriate McLuhan's[132] oft quoted, appropriated and misappropriated phrase "the medium is the message." To this end I will provide a description of the analytic tools to be used and the rationale for their selection.

As already discussed briefly, two 'tools' will be utilised: Guattari's 'schizoanalysis' and Zerzan's 'de-domestication'/'re-wilding'. As far as can be gleaned from a literature review, these two concepts have never been used together in a methodology, thus there is something of the experimental about this arrangement. These concepts will be discussed, shaped and combined (or possibly hashed together) in the following section to create a methodology. In addition to the matter of these tools of analysis three case studies will be explored in-depth. This case study exploration will both use the two tools and also the case studies will act as tools themselves. The methodology section will thus also give a rationale for the choice of these specific case studies and will visit some of the more general issues surrounding the use of case study material in research.

This approach is broadly within the post-structural arena in that it is suspicious of claims to objectivity and/or the raising up an essential a-historical 'subject'. It casts doubt upon Enlightenment beliefs about "language and representation being transparent vehicles for the communication of prior, original meaning and intention" (Davies, Hoggart and Lees)[133]. Post-structural research demonstrates an awareness of the way power (in the micro and macro) operates through discourses and claims to knowledge. This means acknowledging context, milieu and the 'other' often either suppressed or romanticised by dominant/hegemonic discourses[134]. This approach acknowledges that "every research tool or procedure is inextricably embedded in commitments to particular versions of the world" (Hughes)[135]. Guattari is widely seen as falling into the post-structural, most obviously for his critiques of signifying semiotics and Lacan's structural psychoanalysis mapping an underlying essential structure to the unconscious. It should be noted, however, that Guattari, Foucault and Deleuze all rejected the label post-structural despite all having works seen to be within the canon of this movement[136]. Whilst acknowledging the reductive risk of pigeonholing thinkers as prolific as Deleuze and Foucault it must also be borne in mind that post-structuralism is a broad and heterogeneous field and itself cannot be reduced or equated with the "black-hole" of nihilist post-modernism[137]. Schizoanalysis is a post-structural technique in the sense that it abhors rules and absolutes, preferring to find a cartography in flux/flow/movement/becoming. Arguably the most frequent use of post-structuralism in research has been the application of feminist and post-colonial critiques to a wide variety of disciplines.

In spatial theory within human geography, post-structural research in recent decades has owed a debt to the connected domains of the affective, relational and non-representational. These are domains neglected and ignored by more traditional 'rational' and reductive methodologies. Anderson and Smith make a strong case for this in a Transactions of the Institute of British Geographers editorial from 2001: "we have been reflecting on the extent to which the human world is constructed and lived through the emotions. In doing so, we have been forced to confront the glaringly obvious, yet intractable, silencing of emotion in both social research and public life.....this suppression produces an incomplete understanding of the world's workings" (Anderson and Smith)[138]. They go on to suggest that this kind of methodology is "associated with being and doing, with participation and performance, with ways of knowing that depend on direct experience more so than reflection, abstraction, translation and representation"[139]. Since that was written a body of research and method has grown to address this deficit, although it remains a marginal research activity within academia generally. Thrift's development of non-representational theory is an example of the increasing use of complex affect/relational/everyday experiential methodologies[140].

Exploring domains of immanence in research demands an awareness of different spatial and temporal scales, whilst also allowing thought to traverse these scales. The 'everyday' is a scale of immanence within which affect and relationality can be explored in their relentless movement[141]. As stated in my introduction, modernity can be characterised as an "affect on lived experience". This echoes Habermas' idea of modernity 'colonising the lifeworld'[142]. Through my discussion of different definitions of 'modernity' it could be seen that a chronological or 'epochal' definition was not sufficient. If we delineate modernity as a "set of practices that are at the

core of [...] who we make ourselves to be"
(Koopman)[143] then the affect of our routine
'everyday' becomes a credible and valuable point
of study.

To use Thrift's theorising, the way life is put
into practice beyond any cognitive or
representational grid is telling of the everyday,
and particularly how the everyday is
changed/changes. To discuss the everyday is to
enter a scale too often taken for granted and
infused by 'powers' that "make certain aspects of
the events we constantly come across no so much
hard to question as hard to even think of as
containing questions at all" (Thrift)[144]. The
methodological challenge is how to 'crack open'
these questions.

The shock to the old guard of the uprisings of
May 1968 were, arguably, that transversal
connections could be made in the 'everyday' that
'cracked open' hidden/obscured questions and
didn't require a party structure or a vanguard.
Vaneigem captures this in his scathing critique
(published just before the events of May 1968,
making it an interesting comparison to Deleuze
and Guattari's 'Anti-Oedipus' published in the
aftermath) of the alienation and inauthenticity of
the everyday within capitalist modernity:

"Lived experience is always the raw

material of the social contract, the coin in which the entry fee is paid. Life is sacrificed, and the loss compensated through the dazzling manipulation of appearances. The poorer everyday life becomes, the greater the appeal of inauthenticity; the greater the sway of illusion, the greater the impoverishment of everyday life. Ousted from its essential place by the bombardment of prohibitions, constraints and lies, lived reality seems so trivial that appearances get all our attention. We live our roles better than our own lives. Given the prevailing state of things, compensation alone confers weight. The role compensates for a lack: the inadequacy of life – or the inadequacy of another role" (Raul Vaneigem)[145].

SCHIZOANALYSIS

I will now provide an overview of Guattari's concept of Schizoanalysis, followed by Zerzan's theorising around re-wilding and undoing domestication. I will then discuss how a synthesis of the two will be workable in answering the problematic of mental distress in the spaces of modernity. The term Schizoanalysis is first coined by Guattari in essays written in the 1960's and collected in his 1972 work *Psychanalyse et transversalité. Essais d'analyse institutionnelle* (portions of which have been translated into English, but not published together in the same format as this 1972 edition). In the first part of Capitalism and Schizophrenia 'Anti-Oedipus' co-authored with Gilles Deleuze[146] Schizoanalysis receives its first concerted theorization read by a wider audience. This book was their impassioned critique of the reductive, systematised, structured and 'neurotic' constructs that have a hold over subjectivity and which colonise thought and practice in everyday life. Most obviously this was against the 'Oedipus complex' and psychoanalysis, but the critique was far wider reaching. Foucault suggests that anti-oedipus is "an introduction to the non-fascist life" in which Deleuze and Guattari ask how we rid fascism from "our speech and our acts, our hearts and our pleasures.....the fascism that is ingrained in our behaviour"[147]. This is clearly not limited to Deleuze and Guattari's temporal and spatial setting, despite their immanent battles with the French Communist Party, psychoanalysis and state institutions. Schizoanalysis is also not a transcendental or essentialist concept but an immanent "materialist psychiatry"[148].

Against the neurotic, Deleuze and Guattari

pose the breakthrough and flight of the schizo (whilst not denying the risk of 'breakdown' as the schizo line of flight crashes into burn out, representation and repression to become the clinical 'schizophrenic'). "The ethical reversal of schizoanalysis chose *psychosis* as its machinic source and model, instead of the signifying impasse of *hysterical neurosis*" (Polack)[149]. As Seem puts it in his introduction to the English edition of Anti-Oedipus, "a schizoanalysis schizophrenises in order to break the holds of power and institute research into a new collective subjectivity and a revolutionary healing of mankind"[150]. I will dwell on this idea of the 'schizophrenic' deterritorialisation further as this is such a vital point to grasp and is one of the more misunderstood parts of the philosophy of Deleuze and Guattari. This misunderstanding often arises amongst those who personally or professionally spend time with people diagnosed/labelled as Schizophrenic (debates about the validity or values of psychiatric diagnosis aside) and witness the distress experienced in this condition. On first reading of Deleuze and Guattari their championing of the 'schizo' over the 'neurotic' can sound like a crass romanticising of a distressing state, but it must be understood that they are taking these categories out of the restrictive diagnostic manuals or clinical settings and infusing them with and through the 'social' (and in Guattari's later theorising the 'environmental')[151]. The point being that "The schizo is not revolutionary, but the schizophrenic process... is the potential for revolution" (Deleuze and Guattari)[152]. In a way they are returning the political to its excluded place within the domain of affects, taking the schizo out of its reduction in the closed monadic subject of Cartesian idealism and finding it in the multiplicity and the relational subject (My discussion will later turn to elaborate the group/multiplicity/assemblage nature of schizoanalysis). This is first and foremost a critique of the production of subjectivity imposed by inhabiting the milieu of capitalism and modernity, in a secondary fashion, but, inevitably as an institution of modernity and as the site of Guattari's occupation, psychiatry finds itself in the firing line. In summary...

"...for Guattari, schizophrenia becomes the operator of a transformation of the socius that reflects back on modes of social subjectification.

To the extent that it designates the hyletic process that every society gives form to, schizophrenia in the normal sense doesn't only indicate a pathology of capitalism: it becomes necessary to correlate socio-political analysis with a psychoanalysis that has exchanged its reference to the unitary *psyche* for a hyletic flux that requires that one give it the name *schizoanalysis*.

Schizophrenia, then, becomes the generic name for diverse processes of subjectification." (Anne Sauvagnargues)[153].

Numerous claims have been made that Schizoanalysis brings together a variety of philosophical traditions. Sauvagnargues states that Guattari's problematic conjugates the "contributions of Marx, Sartre and Lacan"[154]. Holland suggests that Schizoanalysis is a "reciprocally corrective" synthesis of Marx, Freud and Nietzsche. He characterises the separate and neurotic Libidinal economy (asceticism) of Freud and the political economy (capitalism) of Marx meeting via the schizo flow of 'desiring machines' as desiring production and social production[155]. These 'desiring machines' thus become an essential part of the schizoanalytic artillery, smashing the walls of specialisation to allow connective movement across heterogeneous domains. Desire is a revolutionary methodology in that it is a process rather than a structure or a genesis[156] and to Deleuze and Guattari

Schizophrenia represents the absolutely free, decoded flow of desire[157]. Moving on to the second part of Capitalism and Schizophrenia – A Thousand Plateaus[158] – the phrase "Schizoanalysis" slips into the background amidst a plethora of new concepts and terminology. The theme of Schizoanalysis, however, is not lost as it develops and finds continuance through terms such as 'nomadology'[159] and 'rhizomatics'[160]. This is fitting for a method of analysis which is against fixity, instead requiring a smooth space to make transversal movements across boundaries. Here, amidst the smooth and the striated spaces discussed earlier, to conduct a schizoanalysis requires that we construct a 'nomad war machine' and to find our 'body-without-organs'. Gone are the detailed references to Oedipus found in the earlier edition, but retained is the deterritorialisation of the structured psychoanalytic unconscious and the fight against the repressive 'Oedipalisation' of everything enforced by dominant discourses.

Following and during the publication of the two 'Capitalism and Schizophrenia' books, Guattari devoted much of his solo writing, speaking and activism to the concept of schizoanalysis[161] and to the investigation of what it means to be a 'schizoanalyist'. One thing he is unequivocal about throughout is that it is not "a new special field that would be called upon to find a home within the psych domain"[162]. Partly this is to avoid the re-territorialisation of rigid professionalism/specialisation, which would build up striations and turn an immanent practice rooted in everyday social reality into a self-referential abstraction. To create a new professional domain would be to make "transcendental entities impermeable to concrete situations"[163], this would be to repeat the same problems presented by psychoanalysis and medical psychiatry. Another reason to resist/reject making a new psych specialism out of schizoanalysis is Guattari's rejection of a free-standing essential individual subject and his belief in the efficacy and agency present within assemblages. Bennett defines assemblages, following Deleuze and Guattari, in five points[164]:

1. An historical and circumstantial ad-hoc grouping.

2. "a living throbbing grouping whose coherence coexists with energies and countercultures that exceed and confound it".

3. A web within which power is not equally distributed: an "uneven topography".

4. It is not governed by a central power, its activities and consequences are beyond individual comprehension/competence.

5. "an assemblage is made up of many types of actants: humans and non-humans; animals, vegetables, and minerals; nature, culture, and technology".

Guattari reports that an assemblage is made up of "possible fields, virtual as much as constituted elements, without any notion of generic or species' relation" that are "swept up and reshaped by a sort of dynamism"[165].

This point about schizoanalysis finding its agency and application through assemblages is vital and is possibly *the* major factor that differentiates it from other 'therapeutic practices'. Other practices claim to have a transcendental efficacy with the individual without regard (or with only scant regard) to context/milieu, but often hide complex unseen actants/actors within their functioning. An example of this is the suggestion that the therapeutic benefit of Electro-Convulsive Therapy in some cases may actually reside in the assemblage of inputs and relations across the whole process and not the mechanistic application of an electrical current to the temples of the subject (similar to, but more complex than, the 'Hawthorne effect' and the 'placebo effect'). Schizoanalysis overtly acknowledges and champions this complex (and usually ignored/unacknowledged) interaction of heterogeneous factors present within the assemblage. Guattari experimented with the group (which, it must be noted, is more limited in actants/actors than the assemblage) and the multiplicity in the therapeutic practices at the La Borde clinic. His interest from the early 1960's being institutional therapy with psychotic patients (following François Tosquelles' innovations when working during the Spanish Civil War in Catalonia) rather than the 1:1 work with neurosis characteristic of much Freudian/Lacanian psychotherapy[166]. He differentiates between subject groups and subjugated groups[167], finding ways to maximise transversality, in a similar fashion to the use of a 'grid' to mix up the roles within La Borde and deterritorialise the traditional division of labour within an institution[168].

Having clarified what schizoanalysis is and what a schizoanalyst does by teasing out themes, such as materialist, non-professional, everyday, transversal, revolutionary, group/assemblage, etc, from Guattari's (and Deleuze's) work, I will now conduct a similar exercise for Zerzan's de-domestication and re-wilding.

RE-WILDING

As discussed previously, Domestication is the key problematic and analysis that Zerzan brings to the table. This is not an area ever explored by Guattari, but it can be a fruitful lens through which to realise a project of schizoanalysis. The reason for this is that Schizoanalysis and much of the critique of modernity contained within post-structuralism as a whole is *for* the 'civilised' domesticators and domesticated. Like Guattari (and Zerzan) I am writing from a position within civilisation, having been born in a high-tech urban hospital, weaned on products of agricultural domestication and industrial systems, educated through a typical Western system of specialisation, age segregation and pedagogy and employed in the cash nexus of a capitalist economy. Thus post-structuralism and schizoanalysis is a critique *for me* as a modern subject. I am well versed in a particular symbolic culture in which mind (following Descartes) and language are seen/treated as ontologically superior to embodiment. Modern narratives and modern myths have been the lens through which I have come to know the world and, as a white middle-class male in a developed country, being on a particularly dominant side of the flip of the modernist coin has been the conditioning of my subjectivity. Zerzan's challenge, however, is 'what about the un-civilised? the un-domesticated?' What do those not colonised, or only very recently colonised, by modernity have to bring to the table of critique? If "the cycle of pathology as we know it begins with domestication" (Glendinning)[169] and schizoanalysis speaks to those, like me, who are deep within this pathology, then schizoanalysis has very little to say to the un-domesticated. On the other hand the un-domesticated may have a lot to insert into the critique of modernity and to say to my/our modernist pathology. In this sense Zerzan's work is the reverse of the traditional project of colonisation.

Chellis Glendinning characterises domesticated (including, but not exclusively, modern) society as having a relationship to space composed of detachment, management, control and domination[170]. Through this approach the individual "human psyche came to develop and maintain itself in a state of chronic traumatic distress" (Glendinning)[171] and herein lies the pathology discussed above. I will revisit this concept of whole-culture Post Traumatic Stress Disorder (PTSD) as a novel subversion of psychiatric diagnosis in a later section. This point made by Glendinning about domesticated spaces echoes Lefebvre's 'abstract spaces'[172] of modernity or Auge's homogeneous 'non-places'[173]. This leaves us with the question: What relationship to space can be seen outside of domestication, what way of life, what kind of subjectivity that isn't in a state of chronic trauma? In answering these questions we can begin to see a 'line of flight' that could inform those of us wishing to analyse mental distress in the spaces of modernity.

Zerzan suggests that any critique, if it is to be taken seriously, needs to acknowledge that it (and society) is stuck (for now) within the reification of language and symbolic thought, that these shape the world and the pathological subjectivity that is passively accepted as 'normal'[174]. He characterises this as...

> "...a fall into representation, whose depths and consequences are only now being fully plumbed. In a fundamental sort of falsification, symbols at first mediated reality and then replaced it. At present we live within symbols to a greater degree than we do within our bodily selves or directly with each other" (John Zerzan)[175].

David Kidner has similarly suggested that industrialism is just the most recent manifestation of a problem that stems from symbolic thought[176]. This reliance on symbolic thought folds in on itself in a self-referential totality and develops immensely dysfunctional and damaging 'emergent properties' that are very hard to analyse critically using the specialisms and discourses created within that same symbolic culture[177]. It can be seen that there is considerable (although not complete or uncontested) common ground to be found between Zerzan (and Kidner's) critique of language and the symbolic and the poststructural critique of representation (eg, non-representational theory).

This then is the first point of re-wilding as methodology, to be reflexive and critical of my (and most readers of this piece) situation within a particular symbolic culture. As Mick Smith summarises, drawing upon Bordieu,

> "If we want to move away from modernism, then we cannot ignore the intellectual and moral call to reflect on how our mode of thinking might embody past traditions, present circumstances, and future hopes of modernity. Reflexivity demands that we try to situate ourselves and our thinking in respect to others, to recognise how our theoretical expressions are inscribed within, and are products of,

the practices of our own social formation"
(Mick Smith)[178].

The next point to make about re-wilding is
that, like Guattari's transversality, it must cross
boundaries. The specific boundary to be crossed
here is that between damaged psyche and
damaged nature/ecology/environment. The core
of Zerzan's thinking is about a lost relationship
with the wildness and immediacy of the natural
world and the briefest summary of re-wilding
would be 'the removal of mediations
between/within human collectives and wild
nature' (my words). For Zerzan individual psych-
pathology is inseparable and indistinguishable
from macro-political issues such as mass-
shootings or fracking and from ecological issues
such as climate change and ocean acidification.
His critique demands that we traverse these
issues and remove the specialisms that give us
'blinkers'. I do not dismiss the risks of talking
about 'nature' and the contestation of this
term[179], but do not believe such a fear should
discourage us from engaging with radical
theorists such as Zerzan. Both David Kidner and
Mick Smith also have a wish to 'traverse'
domains and bring 'nature' back into critical
theory/social science discourse through their
work. Kidner building bridges between

psyche/psychology and environment, and Smith building bridges between ethics and spatial theory and environment. They both engage critically with debates around social constructivism and scientific realism, failing to dismiss the insights of either. Their solutions are both richly relational, Kidner taking a broadly 'critical realist' approach to the problematic[180] whereas Smith characterises his approach as an 'antinomian ethics of place'[181].

Zerzan's critique is a radical challenge to bring to the analysis of modernity. He lays down the challenge that civilisation cannot only be analysed and critiqued, but can be actively dismantled. In this sense he emphasises an immanent performative approach to theorising, a belief in the importance of 'anarchy' over and above 'Anarchism'. This suspicion of 'isms' echoes to some extent Guattari's wish to avoid re-territorialising Schizoanalysis as a 'psy' specialism. Anarchy as an approach to critique and to everyday life has pre-figuration as a central tenet, "rather than believing that it is possible to use authoritarian or undemocratic means to create a free and equal society, anarchists have developed ways of embedding the political principles of an envisaged anarchist society into the ways they organise in the here-and-now" (Ince)[182]. Anarchy, and I would argue particularly green/primitivist anarchy, sees wildness as something to be found via practice and relationality. This is similar to Deleuze and Guattari's focus upon 'becoming' and flux. Embodiment is key to this, the sensual affect of seeking out the limits to civilisation's constraints. Rather than (or as well as) a disembodied 'mind' exercise of thinking through the iron bars of the prison cell, re-wilding is the act of removing the cell bars and finding relationality with the 'outside', be this 'wild nature', a heterogeneous community assemblage or the warm flesh of one's lover. This exploration of relationality, affect and practice can be found in much recent poststructural research on space[183]. How, in the everyday, we make space through our practices and how it affects the practices that we partake in offers huge scope for re-envisaging (and expanding) the 'possible'[184] and dismantling that which is pathological. The cold rationality of modernist discourse would want to deny this rich contextuality, as Enlightenment turned out to be a totalising force that seeks to both deny the existence of an 'outside' and destroy any 'outside' (Adorno and Horkheimer)[185]. By acknowledging, as Zerzan does, our domesticated subjectivity and the possibility of an 'outside' of modernity to inform our practice of 're-wilding', this methodology and research can open up an "affective space, which is the space in which we are emotionally in touch – open to the world and aware of its 'affect' on us" (Simonsen)[186].

So, to summarise, Zerzan's concept of 're-wilding' can be opened up as a methodology to explore my problematic of mental distress in the spaces of modernity. I have argued that traits to be drawn from Zerzan's critique are an acknowledgement of the domestication of our subjectivity and discourses as modern subjects and an active reflexivity towards these contexts. Secondly a 're-wilding' methodology will challenge division of labour and rigid specialisations, thereby freely traversing artificial (and often binary) divides such as culture/nature, human/animal, mind/body etc. My final methodological point is that re-wilding is pre-figurative, affective and rooted in practice, meaning that the scope of the 'possible' can be re-envisaged. Overall *the* most important point to take away from Zerzan's work is that there *is* an 'outside' to modernity, however hidden and marginalised that 'outside' has become. To follow Zerzan's line of thinking therefore modernity/Enlightenment as an 'unfinished project' (in Habermas' words) is not in need of 'completion' (in Habermas' theorising), but in need of dragging to the ground and 'finishing off'

with a carefully placed kick (a methodology of
practice)!

CASE STUDIES

This methodology will now become operative through an in-depth exploration of three case studies followed by a specific discussion of mental distress in the spaces of modernity. The case studies have not been chosen for the purpose of making straightforward generalisations that could be transferred 'un-translated' to the context within which I am an actor. As previously discussed this would be beyond the scope of what I could possibly achieve given the constraints of this project. Even if this were possible it would not be desirable given the reductive and possibly disciplinary nature of such a linear transfer of knowledge. The rationale for the selection of these three particular cases is that they are diverse and different from each other and from my context, whilst having some key commonalities. These commonalities are:

1. They all problematize modernity.

2. They all acknowledge an 'outside' to

modernity.

3. They are all concerned with finding different narratives to those that modernity presents as 'normative'.

4. They all have a very strong spatial dimension.

The cases selected are firstly the 'Zapatista' insurgency in the Mexican state of Chiapas, secondly the 'Idle No More' movement of indigenous people in North America and finally the 'Dark Mountain Project' originating in the British Isles. A key point to emphasise is that none of these cases are directly or centrally concerned with mental health, mental illness or psychiatry. This is deliberate and, although some may find it frustrating, healthy to a critique that seeks to traverse specialisms and offer insights from an 'outside' that may be rich with pre-figurative possibility.

The next three chapters will take the case studies one at a time. Each will commence with an introduction to the case/topic/theme being explored, a 'wild schizoanalysis' in the flavour of Guattari and Zerzan will then be applied and the chapter will conclude with implications to be carried forward into my problematic.

CASE STUDY 1: THE ZAPATISTA INSURGENCY

The first of my heterogeneous illustrative case studies is the Zapatista movement of the southern Mexican state of Chiapas. As if it were a plateau in Deleuze and Guattari's "A Thousand Plateaus", this case study has an 'event' that can be very accurately dated. This day, 1st January 1994, has become something of a legend amongst activist networks, a single day on which many have drawn a line in the metaphorical sand to say this is where and when everything changed. To return to Deleuze and Guattari and the Plateaus, this is when a Rhizome broke the surface. 1st January 1994 at the break of dawn was the dramatic 'coming out' into public attention of a rebel army composed of numerous different groups of Mayan indigenous peoples. This was the exact moment, deliberately chosen, when the long negotiated North American Free Trade Agreement (NAFTA) came into force. Conant describes this 'event' as "pure cinematic genius", the dramatic clash of two worlds: "As the clock strikes midnight in Mexico City, President Salinas de Gortari is toasting the North American Free Trade Agreement (NAFTA) and Mexico's much-ballyhooed entrance into the First World. In remote Chiapas, an invisible army has gathered in the mist of highland villages, uniformed in dark colours, faces masked."[187]

In carefully choreographed manoeuvres, different groups leave their villages in the remnants of the Lacandon rainforest to seize and occupy the towns of San Cristobal de las Casas, Ocosingo, Altamirano, Las Margeritas, Oxchuc, Huixtan and Chanal. In these towns they ransack police stations and government buildings, destroying documentation and computers. They build road blocks, demolish bridges and mount a sustained attack on a federal army barracks to take weapons and ammunition. In each of these occupied towns a spokes-person steps forth and reads a document called "The First Declaration of the Lacandon Jungle"[188], which describes the action as the product of 500 years of oppression and introduces them as the Zapatista National Liberation Army (EZLN – in its Spanish acronym). Grievances and demands are listed, and they draw their own line in the sand stating "Ya Basta!" "Enough is Enough!"

The Mexican government dispatched troops and military hardware to commence what would be an intense 12 day war with casualties running into the hundreds. The EZLN fell back from the towns but maintained an occupation of land seized from large ranches and all around the area of conflict signs go up declaring this as "Zapatista Rebel Territory", with its own jurisdiction outside the rule of the "illegal" government in Mexico City. With this unsurprisingly swift and brutal government response, it seems likely that the fatalities would have been much higher were it not for the equally swift intervention of a surprising actor into this assemblage – national and international civil society. Zapatista solidarity protests took place in many cities around the world, including Mexico City, and global media attention was closely following events in Chiapas. Journalists and NGO staff were on site documenting and reporting events as quickly as the Mexican army. With this unwanted and unexpected negative attention the Mexican government declared a ceasefire on 12th January, and the overt shooting war ceased, but many troops and increased military infrastructure remained in the state. Many commentators have attributed this swift solidarity response to the new found reflexivity of the fledgling Internet and the ability to disseminate information outside of mainstream media outlets[189].

Most strikingly, beyond this 'event', the Zapatista movement has managed to sustain its presence both in global thought and solidarity and on the ground in Chiapas state. It has gone through numerous phases of intensity and focus[190] despite an on-going counter-insurgency war carried out by Mexican state troops and paramilitary groups. Soon after the initial dramatic action the Zapatistas held talks with the Mexican Government, leading to the drawing up of the 'San Andreas Accords', in which promises were made to extend Indigenous rights and to amend access to communal lands. These accords were never implemented and numerous alternative challenges have been placed before the government, including marches to Mexico City in 1997 and 2001 and the 'Other Campaign' (La Otra Campana), when a Zapatista delegation visited every state to hold meetings during the 2006 presidential election campaign[191]. Alongside this activity there have been numerous 'Encuentros' (Encounters) held in Zapatista communities, aimed at bringing together diverse groups including a Latin American Indigenous activists meeting, a women's event and global heterogeneous delegations in the "Intercontinental Encounters for Humanity and Against Neoliberalism". Most recently there have been the Zapatista 'Little Schools' attended by hundreds of interested parties from around the world in 2012 and 2013 and the announcement in August 2014 of a 'Carnival Against Capitalism' spanning Christmas and New Year

2014/15. This strand of their activities has been about opening up (or cracking open) dialogues, sharing experiences and developing a sustained critique of the hegemony of Neo-liberal thought and promoting alternatives.

Nail and others have identified a significant shift in Zapatista strategy around the 10th anniversary of the initial uprising. Nail calls this their "constructivist turn"[192]. A declaration was issued raising the level of security and alert in Zapatista communities, followed by three years of relative silence (from the perspective of the global audience) from the movement. All kinds of speculation accompanied this period, including that the movement was fragmenting, preparing for another shooting war or that key figures were in ill health. All of this proved to be unfounded and when the movement re-opened the flow of communiqués it emerged that the period had been spent building 'autonomy'. Having become frustrated with the duplicity and intransigence of 'official' institutions the Zapatistas had got on with building a 'new world within the shell of the old'. Intensive consultations had taken place within and between base communities, the EZLN military wing of the movement had taken a step back and 32 civilian autonomous municipalities came to the fore. There are estimated to be 300,000 people (mostly from indigenous groups

Chol, Tzeltal, Tzotzil and Tojolobal) living within these autonomous zones. These municipalities are called 'Caracoles' after a spiral shell, and they have a system of smaller local 'Good Government Councils' staffed on a 7-15 day rotation meaning that there are no 'professional' politicians or elected 'representatives', but a constantly shifting variety of people engaged in the everyday life of their community[193]. Like Guattari's grid at La Borde clinic, the aim of this system is to prevent specialised ossification of institutions and individuals.

Out of all of the case studies I have selected this is the one with the most documentary material available. The Zapatistas themselves have produced vast quantities of material including radio output and 'Communiqués', mostly distributed through Mexican newspapers and the Internet, the majority of which have been translated into English and numerous other languages. Many of these are penned by the charismatic and mythic figure bearing the pseudonym "Subcomandante Marcos", one of the few Mestizo (white/Hispanic) faces noted amongst the masked rebels on that January day in 1994. He has been misrepresented as the 'leader' of the movement in much mainstream media analysis, a position which is an oxymoron in a movement claiming to be Indigenous, horizontal and non-hierarchical and this characterisation has been strongly rebuffed. His writings have spanned conventional political discourses, manifestos, poetry, novels, children's books and mythic storytelling and have been widely published[194]. Beyond these primary documents there has been a veritable flood of secondary material of variable quality including mainstream media articles, blog posts, books, academic journal articles, video documentaries and creative fiction pieces. This is indicative of the sustained presence of the movement, having lasted 20 years in the public eye and 30 years in total. Also the Zapatistas have proved to be 'transversal' in their crossing of boundaries with the sheer diversity of projects and subject areas that they have had an impact on or become involved in. This quantity of material makes it a challenge to briefly summarise a movement with so many different facets, applications and outside interpretations.

Something that is immediately apparent is that this group differs markedly from other Latin American guerrilla armies, such as the FARC in Colombia or 'Shining Path' in Peru. These groups tend to be overtly Marxist/Maoist and proclaim to be a vanguard intent on seizing state power in a similar fashion to Castro's guerrilla campaign in Cuba between 1956-59. The Zapatistas, however, have been described as post-left and characterised as the first postmodern revolutionary force[195]. Whilst these labels are often crass and simplistic the diversity of communiqués and tactics produced by the movement bear witness to a radical modification of revolutionary thought and praxis[196]. There is a definite poststructural feel to Subcomandante Marcos' writings, in terms of critiquing dominant discourses, emphasising the need to listen to silenced groups such as women and indigenous and lamenting the linear and binary power dynamics challenged and then replicated by past revolutions. He calls theirs "a dreaming revolution" to created "a world in which many worlds fit". For example, from a communiqué of 1999,

> "That is why the Zapatistas are students and teachers. That is why teachers are Zapatistas... It is a work, a mission, a task, something to do, a path to walk, a tree to plant and nurture, a dream to look after....... Speaks of a world where all worlds fit and grow, where the differences of color, culture, size, language, sex and history don't serve to exclude, persecute, or classify, where the variety may once and for all break the grayness now stifling

us." (Subcomandante Marcos)[197].

A number of academics and commentators, including Simon Tormey[198] and Thomas Nail[199], have acknowledged the strong resonances between Zapatismo and Deleuze and Guattari's philosophy. As a speculative aside it is unfortunate that Deleuze and Guattari both died close to the time of the 1994 actions as their reaction may have been informative. Conversely (and, again, speculatively) if Subcomandante Marcos' real identity is (as suggested by a Mexican State 'investigation') Rafael Guillen, an academic at the Universidad Autonoma Metropolitana (UAM) in Mexico City between 1979 and 1984[200], there is a strong possibility that he was exposed to the work of poststructural thinkers such as Foucault, Baudrillard, Deleuze and Guattari.

Having introduced Zapatismo and given some explanation of its distinctiveness from and continuities with other strands of thought I must now justify why it should be used as a case study in my investigation. Firstly it must be emphasised that I am not aiming to generalise from this case by proposing it as a reproducible blue print for action in my part of Western Europe. Brand and Hirsch[201] have examined what use Zapatismo is to envisaging new emancipatory politics in a European context. They conclude that Zapatismo is informative "not by naïve 'copying', abstracted from specific contexts, but by wise resonances"[202]. In this sense "there are no 'Zapatista truths' but stimuli, the effects of which can unfold in specific contexts and discussions"[203]. Thus my investigation shall eschew the desire to extract eternal truths from the case and I will instead seek those 'resonances' and 'stimuli' that can inform an approach to mental distress in the spaces of modernity. So that is a bit more of the 'how' of this case, but I must return to the 'why'? From the introduction it is clear why Zapatismo is distinctive on numerous levels, including as a revolutionary force, as an approach to 'indigenism', as an intersection between theory and practice and as a re-imagination of the role of literature. Infused through this distinctiveness, I believe it represents a fundamental challenge to the dominant discourses that colour everyday life and choices within modernity. Higgins highlights it as "the most organised and convincing challenge to international neoliberalism witnessed so far"[204]. Neo-liberalism being just the most recent and the first global totality of capital's axiomatising project within the wider framing of modernity. This widely perceived significance makes

Zapatismo the case that could not be ignored.

The first point to explore is how Zapatismo (and my second Case Study – the "Idle No More" Movement) is situated within, but also separate from in distinct aspects, an emerging identity around 'indigenism' and indigenous rights. The use of the term 'indigenous' in lay discourse and by groups to self-define is a relatively recent phenomenon and has arisen around a global collective demand for rights and autonomy by non-nationalist/ethnic marginalised groups[205]. The term, although lacking 'official' definition for various reasons, refers to pre-settler original occupiers of land who now make up a minority of a nation's population. These are people who don't identify with nationalist discourses of state sovereignty, but have "primary attachments to land and culture"[206].

> "These are the estimated three hundred million people from four thousand distinct societies, strongly attached to regions that were recently... the world's last 'wild' places. They are those who share the claim to have survived on their lands through the upheavals of colonialism and corporate exploitation. Their unbroken ancestry is not seen as protecting them from the deleterious impacts of industrial and state

ambitions. Their territories are imposed upon by extractive industries; their beliefs and rituals are imposed upon by those who would convert them (or selfishly acquire their knowledge); and their independence is imposed upon by states striving for political and territorial control. They are those people whose position in the modern world is the least tenable" (Ronald Niezen)[207].

Hopefully from this lengthy definition it is clear why indigenism is a key concept to explore if one seeks to understand the Zapatista movement and also to critique modernity more widely. As discussed in the methodology an indispensable point of view to bring to the table of critique is that of those dwelling 'outside' of modernity, from those not or only recently colonised by this pathology (remembering Zerzan's and Glendinning's theories discussed previously). As hinted at in Niezen's definition, indigenous peoples are on the deadly front line of the expansion of modernity[208], indeed they "are increasingly viewed as canaries in the iron cage of modernity" (Niezen)[209]. To continue this canary metaphor, hearing this distress makes one think of the coal miners of not so long ago who would have taken steps to evacuate the mine or to rescue colleagues on seeing the sentinel species in their midst become sick.

The Zapatistas clearly situate themselves as 'indigenous', being majority formed of members of non-Hispanic pre-settler communities, using minority languages rather than the official Spanish of the Mexican state and not uncritically identifying with nationalist discourses (including that of the 1910 revolution led by their namesake Emiliano Zapata)[210]. While criticised by some left and indigenous groups for not primarily engaging with the emerging mainstay of Indigenous Rights discourse through United Nations and other global processes[211], the Zapatistas have had a co-constructive relationship with this wider movement. This has included traversing diverse movements and building connections between disparate struggles. Much indigenous rights dialogue is suspicious (for valid reasons) of integrating with other struggles, especially given the fragility of cultures that have borne the onslaught of colonisation and development for centuries and have ontologies of collectivity quite distinct from modernist/Enlightenment individualist thought. Zapatismo, however, has deliberately allied in co-solidarity (not simply a uni-directional flow of solidarity from 'western' activists to 'developing' communities) with struggles around women's rights, labour, environmentalism and antiglobalization[212]. Beyond this activity Zapatismo has squarely defined itself as a distinctly indigenous movement, having seen the failure and outdated rhetoric of left/Marxist struggles based around defining a group as workers or peasants[213]. This wider focus of struggle, situated both within and beyond indigenism, has shaped the internal autonomy building practices. Communities have been self critical and not just ossified every practice labelled as 'traditional' in order to set it distinctly against normative values of the state. This has included the questioning of patriarchy and the extreme marginalisation of women in traditional day-to-day life (eg, the 10 point "EZLN Women's Revolutionary Law")[214]. Women's co-operatives have been formed, women have been central to EZLN military activities and they participate on an equal footing in the rotating good government councils.

This multi-level co-constructive/solidarity focus and reflective challenging of dysfunctions within as well as beyond is crucial to a critique of modernity and to seeking a pre-figurative beyond. This is the first point I want to explicitly draw out and carry forward into my wild schizoanalysis. The Zapatistas have engaged in lengthy processes to situate themselves in a particular locus of struggle, they see themselves as present in a particular nexus where history meets multiple versions of a future still to be made. This is why they have not uncritically copied the revolutions of the past, have remained on the peripheries of 'official' indigenous struggles in international institutions and have appeared to repeatedly wax and wane like a tide to outside observers. Parts of the struggle could have been judged as a failure but the movement has not shied away from this in the fashion of a political party. This has been a strength that has set them apart from ossified systems of political representation.

Moving on to the next point to be drawn out in schizoanalytic fashion, I will explore the overtly spatial aspect of the Zapatista movement[215]. Despite all of the global attention and information sharing the movement has remained 'rooted' in the centuries-long land struggles of Chiapas as it did on the first day of the uprising. On this day thousands of acres of land were taken and occupied, defended, used and proclaimed as autonomous. Twenty years later many of these occupations remain in place. A space is literally 'occupied' and a movement is constituted through this occupation and daily use of the space. This can be likened to a stemming of 'flows'. As Marcos wrote in 1992 (released in

1994):

"Chiapas loses blood through many veins: Through oil and gas ducts, electric lines, railways, through bank accounts, trucks, vans, boats and planes, through clandestine paths, gaps, and forest trails. This land continues to pay tribute to the imperialists: petroleum, electricity, cattle, money, coffee, banana, honey, corn, cacao, tobacco, sugar, soy, melon, sorghum, mamey, mango, tamarind, avocado, and Chiapaneco blood flows as a result of the thousand teeth sunk into the throat of the Mexican Southeast. These raw materials, thousands of millions of tons of them, flow to Mexican ports and railroads, air and truck transportation centers. From there they are sent to different parts of the world: The United States, Canada, Holland, Germany, Italy, Japan, but with the same fate – to feed imperialism. The fee that capitalism imposes on the Southeastern part of this country oozes, as it has since the beginning, blood and mud." (Subcomandante Marcos)[216].

It is crucial to note that the majority of indigenous people living within Zapatista territory do not have the means to travel to far flung parts of Mexico or would be able to cross international boundaries. They are thus there in a space, with lines of numerous types keeping them in that space. However, by stemming certain flows and reversing others (eg, solidarity visitors from outside) and by removing ranchers' lines and experimenting with line/boundary practices of their own this space has been transformed.

The occupation of space over lengthy periods of time, remembering the pre-settler origins of indigenous identity[217], leads to a relational knowledge of that space. In this sense people are made by their space just as they make their space in a complex co-constitution. Ingold[218] suggests that this interrelation could be called "a poetics of dwelling", in which a knowledge of a space is richly pre-objective, pre-ethical and (my addition), by implication, pre-modern. This type of indigenous knowledge has a non-representational character far richer than a modernist attempt to achieve a scientific 'objective view from a neutral no-where'. It is non-representational (and non-symbolic) in that it is an "intuitive understanding" that "rests in perceptual skills that emerge, for each and every being, through a process of development in a historically specific environment" (Ingold)[219].

Thus space, psyche and subjectivity are intimately co-constituted through their inter weaving with each other. This is what 'rootedness' means in a concrete empirical case, as opposed to the desperately vain appeal to a modern subject to be 'rooted' (in romantic, nostalgic or self-help industry platitudes) in an everyday already colonized by 'abstract spaces of modernity' (to borrow Lefebvre's spatial classification).

Hesketh[220], drawing on the work of Lefebvre, identifies "centrality of space"[221] in the Zapatista movement as indicative of a "clash of spatial projects"[222]. By rejecting the "production of alienated spaces, the Zapatistas have created "counter spaces" in which the production of space is based upon collective need. Collective control is asserted over space, and political activity is associated with everyday life rather than with fleeting privileged moments of "parliamentary cretinism"" (Hesketh)[223]. In drawing parallels with resistance in the neighboring state of Oaxaca, Hesketh suggests that "this reappropriation of space can [...] serve a prefigurative/pedagogical function, demonstrating future possibilities through the collective memory of the creation of alternatives" (Hesketh)[224].

This leads us on to enquire as to specifically

what kind of space it is that Zapatista communities occupy. The majority of communities are low-density and reliant upon small horticultural plots supplying subsistence and some exportable crops. These communities span a mountainous area and are carved out of remnants of rainforest. This area converges with the Guatemalan border and owes as much to Mayan identity pan central America as it does to Mexican identity. As Higgins documents, there is a considerable back story to the Chiapas rebellion covering centuries of different approaches to the indigenous population[225]. This has included times of genocide, religious conversion and land theft, periods when the area has been largely forgotten/overlooked/ignored by central administrations and attempts to integrate indigenous peoples into peasant discourses of land re-distribution. Most recently there has been the arrival of neo-liberal practices through the introduction of NAFTA, this has seen the abolition of article 27 of the Mexican constitution relating to land re-distribution and the loss of protective market mechanisms of commodity prices leading to falling prices for coffee, maize and other exportable crops. It is important to note from Higgins' analysis that NAFTA is merely the immediate trigger cause of rebellion, as the First Declaration of the

Lacandon Jungle states "we are the product of five hundred years of struggle"[226].

The third strand to be drawn out and carried forward into my schizoanalysis is the centrality of myths and storytelling to the Zapatista movement. By doing this I am not moving on from my analysis of space as Zapatista myths are infused with space, just as our modern myths are committed to a particular version of space. Riedner[227] discusses the task of "Writing Zapatismo" by emphasising that the movement is other/subaltern, that its spaces, discourses and communiqués are "culturally outside of exchange value, not intelligible to dominant representations"[228]. She warns of the danger of reading Zapatista material unreflectively in the western university, as a western researcher, with a task to "represent and re-represent the subaltern" into academic discourse[229]. To read Zapatismo therefore requires an openness to a radical affectivity – "As we read, we can choose to enter into the language of others. We can feel moments where our language and ourselves are broken down. We can hear moments in which the concepts and identities in which we ground ourselves are put into question because they are not grounded" (Riedner)[230]. To become immersed in myth is seen as an irrelevantly dangerous (and infantile) pastime by a modernity steeped in the de-mythologising rhetoric of the Enlightenment. But this de-mythologising is itself a "myth of mythlessness", it is the arrogant belief that one's society has "transcended the need for mythical forms of thought" (Coupe)[231]. This belief is arguably more dangerous than willful immersion in subaltern stories and myths because it requires an unacknowledged subscription to modernist myths that have a powerful (and too often genocidal) effect on any subjectivity and ecology that lies outside.

Marcos' writings demonstrate an understanding that "a new way of doing politics requires a new discursive approach" (Di Piramo)[232]. This kind of narrative believes in re-writing the "reality of "what is"" by opening up a space for the "could be"[233]. This is done using numerous techniques, including challenging representation, playfulness, irreverence and demystifying by appealing to the "human and the contingent" (Di Piramo)[234] – in other words with strong resonances in the affective and the everyday practice and performativity of life. As suggested by my previous references to the 'everyday', this is a plane of analysis where there is ready "ontological possibility" (Riedner)[235]. For instance the frequent use of humour by Marcos makes laughter available as a response to reading/hearing and thus "laughter suggests that there are other affects available, and that other meanings can fill our thoughts and emotions"[236]. Modernist discourse rarely invokes laughter as a deliberate response. This discourse may invoke conformity through the quoting of cold data enforcing an 'objectivity' or it may invoke anger or frustration that one cannot be part of or is not living up to an Enlightenment ideal, but rarely laughter. So as a smile appears or a chuckle bursts forth grand narratives of 'progress' are seen for the farce that they are, cracks appear in the colonial project and modernity can appear as just one story among many.

CASE STUDY 2: IDLE NO MORE

The second of my case studies is a movement that has strong resonances with the Zapatistas of Chiapas, but allows us fresh insights and further points to carry forward into a schizoanalysis of mental distress in the spaces of modernity. Its origin was amongst first nations communities in the space commonly known as Canada. It is a movement that, like the Zapatistas, reached its full gestation via the immediate trigger of a piece of legislation and can again be accurately dated. This origin was November 2012, when four women organised a "teach-in" to raise awareness of "omnibus Bill C-45" proposed by the neo-

Conservative federal government led by Prime Minister Steven Harper. The meeting convenors, Sylvia McAdam, Jess Gordon, Nina Wilson and Sheelah Mclean, could have had no idea that their gathering in Saskatchewan would spark a movement with allies around the world and that is still active over three years later. This beginning seems more contingent than the intensive ten-year military preparations of the Zapatistas before their Rhizome broke the surface. Also the stakes do not immediately appear to be as high, with the rebels in Chiapas facing a very real threat of imminent violent death. This contingent and relatively un-dramatic birth should not be misunderstood however. The Idle No More movement shares with the Mayan rebels a lengthy heritage and considerable histories of grievances and injustices as indigenous groups dwelling within settler-colonial states. The Kino-nda-niimi Collective describe it as "this most recent link in this very long chain of resistance"[237]. Again we can hear the echoes of an anger 500 years in the making, but with a very contemporary and concrete expression.

The Bill C-45 that triggered the initial teach-in was passed as the Jobs and Growth Act by the Parliament of Canada in December 2012. Two particular points in this large act specifically sparked concern amongst first nations groups and others. These were Point 4.4 and 4.18 of the Act relating to Fisheries and Navigable waters. These were seen as contravening environmental protections more widely and Native Treaty rights specifically[238]. Native Treaty is a complex issue to convey with brevity and is hard to grasp for someone in a European context. Numerous treaties were signed between the colonial powers/settlers and the extant native/aboriginal population during the 18th and 19th Centuries. The content and motivations behind these treaties ware varied. Motivations included paternalistic protectionism of tribes, especially from incursions by traders across the fledgling US/Canada border. More usually treaties were cynical ploys of land theft and "keeping an eye" on populations by limiting nomadism through establishing reservations. In still other cases the aim was pacification of tribes considered a threat to settlers. Also Enlightenment ideas of social Darwinism were popular and "Savages" were to be "helped" along a linear step-wise trajectory to civilisation. Few treaties explicitly ceded land and resources to the British Crown, many euphemistically 'leased' land or reserved a right to purchase in the future. Reasons for the varied and often conflicting content of treaties include ineffective language translation during negotiations, weighting placed upon oral and written traditions in native and settler cultures respectively and incomprehension of the meaning and applicability of terms such as 'property' and 'communal'. As Gideon states "This colonial policy was "Schizophrenic", in that it appears to recognise the nationhood of Aboriginal peoples on equal footing, all the while expecting Indians to acknowledge the authority of the British monarchy as well as to cede lands as required or requested"[239]. Many groups never signed any treaties with the settler state, or settlement process negotiations are still on-going, and this has raised the distinction of 'treaty' and 'non-treaty' 'Indians'. After decades of campaigning the Constitution Act of 1982 recognised "existing Aboriginal and Treaty rights", but the details of these rights continue to be debated through Treaty settlement procedures. Not all first nations people would consider the Treaty process a legitimate or the most effective way to argue or defend their rights[240] and this is a theme of contestation.

After the initial meeting on 10th November 2012 in Saskatoon further events were held to discuss the legislation and the Twitter hashtag #IdleNoMore became associated with these meetings. The first of many outdoor events took place on 28th November with a rally near the

Ontario legislature in Toronto. So by the end of the first month of activity the name 'Idle No More' had become attached to multiple independent actions across Canada and the United States. Starting on 17th December something that soon became emblematic of the movement was 'flash mobs' doing traditional round dances and drumming in public spaces. These spaces including shopping malls, government buildings and road intersections, such as Times Square in New York City and the Federal Parliament in Ottawa. Solidarity actions took place as far away as Oslo, Norway; London, UK; and Kobe, Japan. The significance of this visible signifier of indigenous culture, banned and suppressed for numerous decades[241], may have been lost on many settler Canadians and European observers. It, however, presented a tangible spectacle, beyond the networking occurring within communities and on social media, in the midst of the consumer spectacle in the weeks before Christmas. The location in abstract modern spaces is significant;

> "The shopping malls built on stolen lands have been the epitome of consumerism, of capitalism, and of keeping up with what society deems necessary in obtaining. The conscious realize that these institutions

are part of the game, a manufactured colonial culture that keeps people tied to predatory consumerism, and the illusion of debt. The very basis of why lands were stolen to begin with" (Nina Wilson)[242].

The re-membering and pre-figurative power of these flash mobs to the movement is expressed in Poetry by Neal McLeod[243]:

"Now the drums
Of our young people
Make new sounds
And tear away, beat by beat
The closed spaces
To create new places
For the ones that come after us"

Other actions that became part of the movement included lengthy fasting by elders, including Chief Theresa Spence of the Attawapiskat First Nation on Victoria Island. Direct actions to block the flows of resources and cause economic disruption also became a part of the movement, with railway lines in particular being targeted.

The source material to draw upon to explore Idle No More as a case study is far more limited than that available for the Zapatista movement.

The major reason for this lack of material is that Idle No More as a name-able movement is so very recent. There is thus very little published academic material in either journals or books taking into account the often lengthy research and publishing time-line. There is considerable primary documentation published via blogs, newspapers, magazines, media sharing, etc, much of the pro-Idle No More material of this nature has been collected in a print edition published in 2014[244]. Clearly further interpretations and perspectives will emerge as the dust settles or as the movement twists and turns in the coming decades, as has happened with 20 year retrospectives on the Zapatistas. These factors make this a significantly different Case Study to use and to analyse. This is not necessarily a problem as long as it is borne in mind that there is a certain contingency inevitable in this schizoanalysis. This particular deterritorialisation is fresh. It has not been fully re-territorialised or axiomatised (despite efforts/moves to do both). It is a line of flight that remains 'in-flight' for the time being. Also I would argue that Idle No More has more immediate heterogeneity than the Zapatistas as it has no centralised plan or process as the Chiapas rebels did in 1994. 'Official' Idle No More documents have been released, such as the

'Manifesto' in 2013[245], but mostly the movement operates in a decentralised manner, has no 'official' governance processes and individual actions are organised on an autonomous local basis. This decentralisation is partly facilitated by Internet tools such as social media, but it must not be forgotten that First Nations communities have a strong heritage of oral culture, small-scale autonomous governance and contingent collaborative relationality with other First Nations, indigenous and settler groups. Similar debates about the role of social media in facilitating protest and movement building have been debated at length recently in the context of the so-called 'Arab Spring' and the Occupy movement[246]. There is definite association, but it is hard to attribute clear causation, and it would be premature and reductionist to swiftly attribute too much credit to the Internet in these cases.

Beyond the trigger of the Bill and despite its passing into law, the Idle No More movement continued beyond that winter in 2012. The manifesto of the movement states that the "imposition of these bills is in direct violation of the Treaties and the Treaty Relationship" and that "we have laws older than this colonial government about how to live with the land"[247]. Nina Wilson[248] explains that a process of internal colonization has been on-going whilst primacy has been given to a "superficial" official approach using the written words to cede native control of land, resources and sovereignty. This, she argues, belies the nuance and context of the lengthy verbal negotiations which are (and would at the time of negotiation) given a greater weighting/primacy in primarily oral cultures. This fundamental mis-match between native and settler interpretations of treaties and the resultant "internal colonisation" (of which Bill C-45 is only the most recent example) are arguably the key factors of grievance to understand the rise and urgency of the Idle No More movement. Wilson defines internal colonisation in the words of James Tully as "the appropriation of land, resources and jurisdiction of indigenous peoples, not only for the sake of resettlement and exploitation [...] but for the territorial foundation of the dominant society itself"[249]. This clash has been played out in various forms throughout the project of colonialism and it is emblematic of profoundly different ontological and epistemological beliefs of native and Western societies[250]. Glen Coulthard characterises this as a spatial verses a temporal orientation, with indigenous cultures holding lands-places as having the "highest possible meaning" whilst Western societies "derive meaning from the world in historical/developmental terms, thereby placing time as the narrative of central importance"[251]. This echoes the wider problematic of modernity, with Lefebvre's 'abstract spaces' as empty vessels waiting to be filled, and all the developmental logic implicit in this. Abstract spaces being 'developed' therefore "operate[d] as hegemonic spaces promoting the reproduction of colonial order in everyday life" (Larsen)[252]. Settler society is thereby seen as an abstract naturalised norm to which Indigenous ontologies are subsumed and then expected to reproduce in a banal 'biopower'[253]. Thus a settler Canadian society which in late modernity opens an individualistic 'rights' narrative to indigenous communities, offering assimilation as its gift, believes the delusion that the "native issue" is resolved. This 'giving' of a Western/modernist ontology with one hand is accompanied by a thoroughly modernist 'taking' of a healthy bio-diverse un-enclosed land base with the other hand. Herein lies much (but not all) of the explanation for the Idle No More movement and the perplexed and hostile response from many quarters within settler society.

Having introduced the movement and orientated the reader, I will move on to explore the significance of the use of non-settler names, rhizomatic organisation, blockades of flows and healing of trauma as part of a process of de-colonisation. In my schizoanalytic discussion of Idle No More as a case study the theme, introduced in the previous paragraph, of being distinctly outside of modernity will be frequently revisited. As a case study this is illustrative of the existence/possibility of a domain outside of modernity as "The movement exhibits a post-Cartesian Indigenous ethos where the mind, body, spirit, and emotions are engaged together" (Nanibush)[254]. Herein can be seen an overtly spatial engagement of the 'affective', the 'non-representational' and the 'relational' colliding in an 'everyday' that is currently colonised by practices of 'biopower'. If my premise (see introductory chapter) of the dis-ease characterising modernity is applied to this context one can see the insights available from those only recently colonised by this pathology. This is therefore an illustrative point where Zerzan's critique of domestication can be 'hashed' with Guattari's analytic to begin to work out what a "wild schizoanalysis" will/could look like when brought back to bear on mental distress in the spaces of modernity.

De-colonisation is both a process and an aim. It is the "colonized, exerting themselves against ongoing cultural and economic hegemony"[255]. As a process, de-colonisation is an unmasking of the violence that the colonial project masks/justifies as progress via reason. This is a violence not just of armies and government institutions but of ways of thinking that naturalise the settler's ontological/ epistemological assumptions[256]. For a schizoanalytic methodology this process "entails deconstructing the discursive edifice that has resulted from the confluence of 'western' knowledge-building and empire-building, and an undermining of hegemonic forces that keep it in place" (Shaw, Herman and Dobbs)[257]. I suggest that the widespread practice within the Idle No More movement of rejecting settler names and re-naming is a decolonizing ploy that is deliberately "semiotically disruptive" (Genosko)[258]. This is most obviously seen in the refusal/reluctance to use the words "Canada", "America" or "United States" when describing the spaces and places of habitation and action. Thus the idea is suggested that "continents are not natural spaces, but projects that rely on specific notions of spatiality" (Maldonado-Torres)[259]. When describing the wider continent beyond individual First Nations territories, the term "Turtle Island" is employed. Turtle Island refers to a creation myth from the oral cultures of the Iroquois and the Ojibwa nations among others. This term is used north and south of the US/Canada border, in fact the border does not exist to this naming schema. This reflects the historic movement of First Nations communities, both in the nomadic way of life and also in migrations/displacements west and north as the fledgling settler states expanded. Thus flows, trails, paths and features of the physical geography are seen as defining the space and not the recently added line/bordering practices indicating the political foibles of the settler states. This is a linguistic/semiotic smoothing of the striations imposed by the bureaucratic state form; showing how "a striated space may be smoothed over or 'dissolved' by the discontinuation of a certain coding operation or by the reintroduction of smooth elements resisting containment or evading certain subordinations" (Genosko)[260].

These two opposing naming schemas could be characterised as different "Regimes of Signs" and, by making the 'major' language of the settler state redundant, First Nations are pre-figuring a de-colonised space in which the official (or any) "language never has universality in itself" (Deleuze and Guattari)[261]. This de-colonial naming is also in evidence at different geographic and personal scales. An example of this, starting in January 2013, is the overlaying of Anishinaabemowin names over signs within the city of Toronto. This is called the "Ogimaa

Mikana Project" and includes street names and tourist sites. One such overlaid tourist sign reads (English translation adjacent to the Anishinaabemowin language):

"Toronto (Place where the logs flow);
We all live on native territory,
Our Anishinaabe Land,
Welcome to our community,
How do you recognize it?"
(The Ogimaa Mikana Collective)[262].

Finishing the sign with a question seems to be both an invitation and a provocation, as is the common use of the term "Unceded xxxx Native Territory" instead of or alongside the Canadian/US place name on postal addresses. Naming actions also take place on the personal level, with the use of names originating from someone's culture rather than the European format of Christian name followed by surname that became common in the "Indian registry" founded in the early 1950's as part of the divisive "Indian Act"[263]. Christi Belcourt emphasises that this re-claiming names must go beyond the point of romantic comfort for settler Canadians; "most Canadians are quite comfortable, and even comforted, by the names of the places they call home that are Indigenous in origin – *but only to a point.* As long as they are in name only and don't come with the burden of acknowledging Canada's past colonialist history and the erasure of past Indigenous ownership of lands"[264]. This is the radical point of re-naming and a sentient reminder of the risk of essentialising a romanticised indigenism into an axiomatic that swallows up the de-colonial line of flight. As Melody McKinver writes "Anishinaabemowin is a complex language and learning it, like decolonization, can't happen overnight. But for both, it is essential that the work be put in."[265].

Moving on from de-colonising actions on the linguistic signifying plane another part of the Idle No More movement is the blockade. This refers to the physical blocking of flows to cause direct economic losses to the settler state. These actions included the "Swamp Line 9" blockade in Hamilton, Ontario, which aimed to stop the movement of Tar Sands output through Ontario and Quebec. This action ended with a large and costly police operation on 26th June 2013. Also numerous days of action took place across the country, such as on 16th January 2013 when numerous rail lines and significant roads, including the Windsor-Detroit international border crossing, were stopped for periods of time. The Enbridge and other pipelines transporting crude oil have also had their operation disrupted during days of action. The overt focus of much of this action is the accusation that the Canadian state is expropriating resources from territory to the detriment of the environment and with paltry compensation to the communities that have used and occupied these territories for thousands of years. This resource extraction includes the large scale clear cutting of forests, especially in the state of British Colombia[266], the vast tar sands fields in Alberta and elsewhere and the damming of rivers[267] and flooding of valleys. DruOja Jay argues that, contrary to a widespread narrative that First Nations communities live off large government subsidies, the net calculation would put subsidies flowing in the other direction[268];

> "Canada's economy could not have been built without massive subsidies: of land, resource wealth.... These industries are taking place on an Indigenous nation's traditional territory, laying waste to the land in the process, submerging, denuding, polluting, and removing. The human costs are far greater; brutal tactics aimed at erasing native peoples' identity and connection with the land have created human tragedies several generations deep" (DruOja Jay)[269].

The blockade as a response to such damage and devastation could be seen as taking the battle to the coloniser's field of representation. Thus if a settler colonial epistemology gives primacy to linear 'progress' and 'development' via numerical representations on a balance sheet, then the blockade acts on this representation by aiming to make a subtraction from said balance. The blockade clearly has qualitative and relational significance beyond this battle on the coloniser's quantitative level of representation, but this is arguably the factor that gets the action widespread attention.

Having attended to the use of re-naming and blockades as de-colonial practices, my analysis will now move on to the area of historical trauma and de-colonial perspectives on healing. This domain arguably falls closest of all the case study analysis to my problematic of mental distress. While I welcome this relevance I would also strike a note of caution. Just as I suggested that a clumsy transfer of Zapatismo to a European context would be unhelpful and unworkable, an un-reflexive transfer of Indigenous experiences of trauma to the mental distress experienced in a European context would be equally problematic. Not least this would resound with cultural expropriation, a practice tightly bound up with the colonial experience. Thus, as with Zapatismo, cautious resonances will be sought.

Indigenous people around the world have disproportionately borne the darker side of modernity. As Bodley titled his book on the subject, Indigenous people are "Victims of Progress"[270]. This is plain to see on the physical environment plane with ample evidence of such things as unsafe supplies of water[271], depleted populations of animals and plants for traditional hunting and gathering practices and ill effects caused by exposure to industrial chemicals[272]. It is widely documented that health outcomes are significantly worse in Indigenous communities in the USA and Canada compared to settler populations[273]. What is also in evidence, however, is significant destruction on the planes of culture and integrity of psyche. The colonisation of the American continents as well as being a physical genocide of indigenous people through deaths via settler aggression and spread of disease was also a cultural genocide. In Canada this cultural genocide took numerous forms including assimilation through the widespread establishment of residential schools for indigenous children. "These schools were created as deliberate agents of cultural assimilation for generations of Aboriginal pupils, whose attendance was mandated by the federal government" (Gone)[274]. The overt ideology of such a system, in some kind of European exceptionalist social-Darwinist delusion was "to kill the Indian and save the man" (Adams)[275]. Experiences within these institutions included suppression of languages other than English and French, enforced participation in Christian doctrines, corporal punishment and sexual assault.

Taking the effects on the physical environment along with effects on culture and psyche, as such domains are inseparable when approached in a non-Cartesian fashion, there is a huge legacy of trauma and distress. Many of the texts coming from the Idle No More movement[276] attest to this cultural devastation, particularly the tragic stories of residential schools. Addressing this trauma through healing is one of the most urgent calls of the movement. As Sarah Hunt states in the context of violence against First Nations women, "communities cannot be self-governing until members of those communities are well"[277]. To recognise the need for healing and to identify paths towards that healing is a potent point that I will carry forward. Nina Wilson attests that "The essence of the movement is not about gender, class, race, belief, etc., it is about healing" and she goes on to express the distinctly spatial aspect of this –

"there can be no healing when our people are still displaced, removed from the land"[278]. Joseph Gone and others in the past decade have explored the notion of 'Historical Trauma' or 'Soul Wound' as a more complex and relational term that expresses the cumulative and intergenerational nature of the widespread experience of dysfunction and distress[279]. This concept deliberately eschews being reified by classification or the risk of distress being 'captured' by the more individualistic and linear notion of Post-Traumatic Stress Disorder (PTSD) classified in the psychiatry manuals International Classification of Disease 10 (WHO 1992) and Diagnostic and Statistical Manual V (APA 2013). This eschewing is vital for Indigenous searches for healing because medical/psychiatric notions of mental health have traditionally been part of the process of colonisation[280]. Despite their claims to universality psychiatric reifications of distress are "ethno-theories" specific to modernity[281], for example "DSM exists, and was developed, in a very specific cultural environment, and therefore may not be applicable to people who live in other contexts" (Nelson)[282].

Thus the search for healing takes us into the domain of space and culture, a theme that will be expanded in later chapters. In this context cultural revitalisation through participation and re-membering is being explored in many communities as a healing strategy. This includes participation in traditional ceremonies[283] and expressing health through concepts which capture a First Nations epistemology such as the medicine wheel[284]. These concepts are relational, non-anthropocentric and acknowledge the importance of space by engaging with landscapes as "therapeutic"[285]. These practices of healing are rooted in the flows of the everyday, rather than being separated in a specialist site of treatment such as a clinic or hospital, and the landscape is not reified in a Western sense – the land being "not just seen as shaping or influencing identity, but being an actual part of it" (Wilson)[286]. In this way, by the negative of refusing western models of health and treatment and the positive of re-building indigenous approaches, healing becomes a radically insurrectionary de-colonial practice. This de-colonial approach to healing will be carried forward into my schizoanalysis of mental distress in the spaces of modernity in a later chapter.

CASE STUDY 3: THE DARK MOUNTAIN PROJECT

"It is, it seems, our civilisation's turn to experience the inrush of the savage and the unseen; our turn to be brought up short by contact with untamed reality. There is a fall coming. ... We do not believe that everything will be fine. We are not even sure, based on current definitions of progress and improvement, that we want it to be." (Kingsnorth and Hine)[287].

The third and final case study that I will pass through a wild schizoanalysis is The Dark Mountain Project. The above quote is from the project's opening salvo, their 19 page manifesto, penned by Paul Kingsnorth and Dougald Hine and published in 2009. Dark Mountain is a clearly defined project as opposed to a movement like the previous two case studies. At its most basic the project is primarily to encourage and be a vehicle for what they call "uncivilised writing" (and art) and their manifesto is intended to create a "spark" for literature that grapples with the end/outside of civilisation[288]. To this end their core activity is to publish and distribute two anthologies of writing and art per year. However, in a similar fashion to Idle No More, Dark Mountain has expanded in numerous and unexpected directions outside and beyond these anthologies. I will return to this later because firstly I should introduce the Manifesto and the concept of "Uncivilisation" more fully.

The manifesto is based on the premise that civilisations have risen and fallen in the past and that our global industrial civilisation is no exception to this rule. Kingsnorth and Hine suggest that the expiration date for this civilisation may well be fast approaching and that very few people/organisations/institutions are engaging seriously with this. These two project founders, particularly Paul Kingsnorth, have a strong heritage in the 'green' movement within the UK and they suggest the collapse of civilisation is not on the mainstream agenda of this movement. The manifesto includes an exasperated critique that the green/environmental movement has reduced itself to simply counting and cutting carbon to the exception of all else; "Today's environmentalists are more likely to be found at corporate conferences hymning the virtues of 'sustainability' and 'ethical consumption' than doing anything as naïve as questioning the intrinsic values of civilisation"[289]. In other words a line of flight that initially may have represented a radical de-territorialisation, as Guattari seemed to hope of the greens in the early 1990's, has been captured and axiomatised by the globalising capitalist project.

Returning to their premise; the authors, assessing civilisation, attribute fragility to what seems a strong construction in the age of its global reach. Beyond the steel and concrete of the cities and their connecting infrastructure civilisation "is built on little more than belief: belief in the rightness of its values; belief in the strength of its system of law and order; belief in its currency; above all belief in its future"[290]. Their analysis is that as soon as the modernist faith that "History becomes an escalator, and the only way is up"[291] is seen as a myth, and a myth that is crumbling, then "the collapse of a civilisation may become unstoppable"[292]. The "myth of progress" is how they sum up this faith or belief that is behind the totality of global industrial civilisation, with its distinct ontologies that are normalised/naturalised into everyday lived reality.

> "The machine is stuttering and the engineers are in panic. They are wondering if perhaps they do not understand it as well as they imagined. They are wondering whether they are controlling it at all or whether, perhaps, it is controlling them. ... Draw back the

curtain, follow the tireless motion of cogs and wheels back to its source, and you will find the engine driving our civilisation: the myth of progress" (Kingsnorth and Hine)[293].

The concept of the myth of progress is a seam that runs through all the activity that falls under the umbrella of the Dark Mountain Project. This resonates strongly into my enquiry as I have previously stated the development of psychiatry beyond the 'bad old days' of the asylum is a myth of progress. Their response to the critique of civilisation that they develop is to encourage and facilitate the distribution of "Uncivilised writing". Their rationale for this is that "trapped inside a runaway narrative"... "Creativity remains the most uncontrollable of human forces: without it, the project of civilisation is inconceivable, yet no part of life remains so untamed and undomesticated"[294]. They state clearly that this is definitely not nature writing or political writing, not "from the self-absorbed and self-congratulatory metropolitan centres of civilisation but from somewhere on its wilder fringes"[295], "outside the stockades we have built"[296]. Particularly this art loses the assumed anthropocentrism of the "siren cries of metrovincial fashion"[297], the "prejudices of the placeless, transnational elite"[298]. To create an uncivilised writing and art is to be relational, to know the world is "something we are enmeshed in", and through this it is "humble, questioning, suspicious of the big idea and the easy answer"[299].

Over the intervening five years, the project has maintained a frequently updated blog, directly published two book length anthologies per year, as well as a compilation album of music. In addition to this an annual weekend festival took place, once in Denbighshire and three times in Sussex, between 2010 and 2013. The reception of the manifesto and the ideas of the project has varied widely. The large amount of submissions for the anthologies and activity level on the project's on-line community suggests it has found adherents/comrades by sparking an interest or tapping into a stream of thought. It has also been negatively received in many quarters, a common criticism being that it represents a nihilist 'throwing in the towel' of any attempt to change the world for the better[300]. An early example of this was a debate between Paul Kingsnorth and the left wing/environmental activist and Guardian columnist George Monbiot. This debate was on-going and included a face to face engagement at the 2010 festival in Llangollen and a full page printed in The

Guardian newspaper on 18th August 2009.

The main thrust of the critique presented by Monbiot is that the collapse of civilisation can and should be resisted as after a fall history tells us that psychopaths would take charge and violence would ensue. He proposes that "a defanged, steady state version of the current settlement might offer the best prospect" and "all we've got and all we've ever had" is the "uncertainty" of "join up, protest, propose and create"[301]. Kingsnorth rebuts this criticism with the assertion that Monbiot is leaving the "founding myths" untouched, that "a retooled status quo is a fantasy" and that

> "The challenge is not how to shore up a crumbling empire with wave machines and summits, but to start thinking about how we are going to live through its fall, and what best we can learn from its collapse" (Kingsnorth)[302].

Monbiot's line of thinking seems to be a relatively common response to the Dark Mountain Project. This is understandable given that large parts of the green movement are invested in the kind of campaigning and lobbying that Hine and Kingsnorth suggest is a delusional diversion. John Zerzan has also critiqued the

Dark Mountain Project, which may seem surprising given his radical anti-civilisation approach. Although he would advocate a future without civilisation, a primitive future (not using primitive in its often pejorative sense), his criticism is strikingly similar to Monbiot's in that he gives agency to humans to make a better future happen (although Zerzan's and Monbiot's images of this future are very different). Zerzan and Monbiot attribute, possibly unfairly, a resignation in the Dark Mountain Project that change for the better is now too late and all that can be done is an adjustment of our narratives to make sense of the world as civilisation collapses around our ears. While this criticism levelled against the project may be true to some extent, the heterogeneity of the contributions and nuance of Hine and Kingsnorth's manifesto are forgotten. The critics miss the point that the project is broad enough to provide a home for adherents to philosophies similar to both the socialist environmentalism of Monbiot and the post-left anti-civilisation anarchism of Zerzan as well as many shades between and beyond these positions. As Hine states in a blog post dated 31st October 2012 "we have been able to bring such a range of voices into conversation: from Wikileaks hackers to Luddites, from bankers and hedge fund managers to survivalists and primitivists, not to mention one Guardian columnist, and one infrastructure engineer who has advised both anarchist squatters and the Pentagon" (Hine)[303]. The anthologies, blogs and festivals, etc, include calls to protest, to insurrectionary direct action, to re-wild, as well as expressions of dejection, mourning, loss and powerlessness. The Scottish author and activist Alastair McIntosh was an early ally of the project and, I would argue, better exemplifies what the Dark Mountain Project is in essence. He has long argued for the affective, spiritual and relational aspects of environmental degradation to be acknowledged and not subsumed beneath a technocratic reductionist reading of climate change[304]. This is what unifies the project and its 'emperors new clothes' enunciation about the Myth of Progress, not some kind of dejected giving in.

A helpful step to contextualise the Dark Mountain Project and to commence a schizoanalysis of it would be to compare and contrast it with another work that was published around the same time. This work is "The Coming Insurrection" by The Invisible Committee, the English language edition of which was published in 2009 following the original French in 2007. This short book is also something of a manifesto penned at the point of crisis when things seem to have reached a singularity. From its opening sentence one can hear the feeling of being on a precipice and looking down, as Uncivilisation invites us to do[305],

> "From whatever angle you approach it, the present offers no way out.... From those who seek hope above all, it tears away every firm ground. Those who claim to have solutions are contradicted almost immediately. Everyone agrees that things can only get worse. "The future has no future" is the wisdom of an age that, for all its appearance of perfect normalcy, has reached the level of consciousness of the first punks" (The Invisible Committee)[306].

However, as opposed to a fragility, a totality is being described that infuses everyday and appears to offer no way out. The widespread loss of faith in a future is acknowledged and the insurrection is said to be inevitable. This, however, is not a glorious revolution of the proletariat vanguard that continues the evolutionary unfolding of history. It is an exasperated insurrection at the point of collapse, progress no longer holds its assurances of better to come, we stand on this dark cliff edge that modernity has delivered us to and dare each other to look down. This sits [un-]comfortably within the tradition of The Frankfurt School and much Critical Theory, in that these movements/theories broadly asked the question of why the Marxist/Hegelian teleos failed to unfold and deliver the progressive future.

The Coming Insurrection received a dramatic response from the French establishment, and others around the world when translations were released. Most dramatically this included twenty arrests on one day in 2008, including the "Tarnac 9" arrested when 150 anti-terrorism police raided a commune near the small village of Tarnac in the Limousin region[307]. A member of this commune was a suspected member of "The Invisible Committee", the anonymous authors of the book. Charges were brought relating to direct action sabotage attacks on high speed rail routes which had caused delays and disruption on numerous occasions. Alberto Toscano puts these arrests down to the notion of "pre-terrorism" − the "repressive pre-emption" of the "imagination of future revolts"[308]. It is obvious that this response differs markedly from that received by the publication of "Uncivilisation", which seems like a polite academic debate in immediate comparison.

Points of similarity between the two manifestos are the evident frustration with metropolitan solutioneering couched in the language of a progressive urbanism. Here we have the most obvious spatial implications of the two. The Coming Insurrection discusses urban flows repeatedly, identifying the 'network' as both the mode of making the totality 'everywhere' and also its unmaking in being the focus for targeted sabotage, using its weak nodes to seed its own destruction[309]. "Nowadays sabotaging the social machine with any real effect involves reappropriating and reinventing the ways of interrupting its networks" (The Invisible Committee)[310]. As discussed above The Dark Mountain project manifesto also rejects this championing of the urban, preferring what is left of the wilder fringes and the forgotten places of empire. Both of these manifestos are thus re-wilding from within, largely written and acted out by those deep within the pathology of civilisation, but with a keen eye to an 'outside' that hasn't been colonised by this pathology or that is loosening the colonising grip. They are both insurrections, at the point where 'progress' has so obviously failed, Dark Mountain being an insurrection on the mythic and narrative plane and The Coming Insurrection on the physical plane of sabotaged flows. In this sense both are pre-figurative of what could be beyond this impasse. As soon as I have written this dichotomy, however, I want to challenge it by saying that both manifestos contain elements of each other's strategies whilst remaining non-reducible to each other. Both are insurrectional with both the pen/keyboard and the monkey wrench. The theories cannot be separated from the action on the ground, there is a two way feedback and modification process, this is a 'live' pragmatics of collapse.

From this comparison with a concurrent manifesto I hope that some clarity has been achieved as to where to situate the Dark Mountain Project. This is the first step of my schizoanalysis of the project and it begs the question as to why similar questions would be asked at the same time. The premise that an end point has been reached, an echo of the Zapatistas' cry that 'Ya Basta – Enough is Enough', is an obvious starting point. 'Uncivilisation' was published at the height of a financial crisis, when the media was full of stories of contraction, recession and the banking system teetering on the 'edge'. Writing in 2015 this particular tone has passed from the media and what is left is a banal parroting of an 'austerity' mantra. From this angle the crisis appears as just another 'crisis of capitalism', the cash continues to 'flow' out of ATMs, house prices appear to rise again and no-doubt some would like to resign the narrative of 'Uncivilisation' to the same cabinet as the nay-sayers of the 1970's oil crisis. This, however, forgets the affective experience of daring to look over the edge. In this sense the experience of living daily within a crisis is largely unchanged since the 1970's, neo-liberalism may have grown to become the hegemonic narrative, but the pathology of 'progress' is much the same. One way of approaching this is through the critique of technology and technological rationality. The Dark Mountain Project has encouraged and hosted this criticism and mistrust of technological solutions. As Kingsnorth and Hine summarise at the end of the manifesto "We reject the faith which holds that the converging crises of our times can be reduced to a set of 'problems' in need of technological or political 'solutions'"[311].

The wider project of technological development is not generally questioned in common discourses, the assumed position being that technology is 'neutral' until it is placed into the 'wrong' hands or concerns generally gravitating around the possible deleterious impacts of individual devices or techniques. This ignores, however, the totality and organisational assumptions necessitated by the everyday functioning of what Jacques Ellul called "the technological society"[312] in which 'technique' becomes total beyond the deployment of individual machines. Thus the problem becomes that "there is just nowhere in the great chain of decision making within a technological society where these kinds of questions get asked, where the deleterious experiential effects of replacing wild others with machines and commodities is properly considered – precisely because the pattern of technology itself sets the terms of the discourse" (Fisher)[313]. Interactions and everyday activities come to be mediated through technologies that are taken for granted or not even seen at all; "This rationality establishes standards of judgement and fosters attitudes which make men ready to accept and even to introcept the dictates of the apparatus" (Marcuse)[314]. This is substantially why the statement above from Uncivilisation about refusing to reduce the crises of our times to 'problems' needing 'solutions' is a radical assertion. To believe that the problems we are seeing with climate change and loss of biodiversity will be solved by inventions/innovations further 'downstream' is to ignore or forget that the problems have a source 'upstream'. Technological rationality, having become normalised into common discourse as suggested above, demands that the issues are approached in this manner and that linear progress will prevail. To discuss the issues as having an 'affective' dimension; or to raise the question that the envisaged 'downstream' solution is no more desirable than the 'upstream' origin of the problem; or even to suggest that such simple linear causation cannot explain the crisis anyway, brings us into the kind of domains that the Dark Mountain Project is attempting to give expression to.

As an interesting vehicle for this technological questioning, the early years of the Dark Mountain project coincided with the bicentenary of the [in]famous Luddite actions. This collection of machine breaking activities largely took place in the English midlands and the main thrust of which took place between 1811 and 1813. There were Luddite related commemorations and discussions at a number of the weekend Uncivilisation festivals. The Luddites are an example of a movement that has strongly entered into mythic narrative, from the common use of the mocking suggestion that someone slow to adopt new technologies is a 'luddite' through to groups labelled (either by self or other) as neo-luddite. I would like to suggest that to engage with the Luddites is to investigate a 'minoritarian' history in the sense that Deleuze and Guattari highlighted the opposition between the 'royal' (major) science and the 'nomad' (minor) science[315]. Iain Boal emphasises this 'minoritarian' voice by likening the Zapatistas to the Luddites in the sense of what E P Thompson called "history from below"[316]. By drawing upon a characterisation of the Luddites as 'minoritarian' and 'from below' I am illustrating why they are a significant movement for an 'uncivilised' art to engage with. By this I mean that what was a movement largely of common people that at the time represented a significant threat to the state bureaucracy and technological development has been frequently ignored, played down or poked fun at. As Kirkpatrick Sale documents in his history of the movement, the numerous Luddite armies operating from Leicestershire through to Lancashire and Yorkshire were very well organised and disciplined. These groups were capable of inflicting damage costing hundreds of thousands of pounds (a considerable sum in 1812), operating for numerous years over a large span of territory and establishing strongly in the popular psyche[317]. To understand their significance and the potent threat they posed to the establishment at the time Sale points out that [their threat] "called forth the greatest spasm of repression Britain ever in its history used against domestic dissent"[318]. This included "spies and special constables, volunteer militias and posses, midnight raids, hanging judges, harsh punishments, and a force of soldiers stationed in the troubled regions greater even than that which had sailed to Portugal with Wellington to fight Napoleon's armies four years before" (Sale)[319]. The scale of this situation represents a potent example of rhizomatic resistance, not just to state actors and early capitalist employers, but to the very notion of 'progress' and what the affect of this was on people's everyday experience. Remembering Ellul's diagnostic of totalising 'techniques' coming to be more significant than individual machines[320], the artisans who were the 'Luddites' were concerned about the death of their cottage enterprises with some level of autonomy at the hands of massive mills, with their shifts, rules and commodification of labour. These new techniques disembedded[321] their skills from the level of community and reified livelihood into something considerably different.

The illustrative use of the Luddite actions is telling of a project that wishes to find narratives that are outside that of progress. Urban space arises as a battlefield or domain of contestation in these two periods. The Luddites in the Industrial Revolution finding themselves in a rapidly urbanising society, their lives being re-shaped/deterritorialised by the spaces required by the totalising 'technique' of machine centred mass industries. The Dark Mountain project from within a culture of changing urbanism, of gentrification and 'cosmopolitan' boom of places such as London's commercial centre; of rapid global urbanisation in places outside the spread of early industrialism, such as South-East Asia; and of urban decay in old industrialised centres such as Detroit and Liverpool. This is not a simple concern with the effects/affects of urbanisation that too often belie a false dichotomy, an opposition between city and country, forgetting that within (particularly European) modernity what is called 'countryside' is in practice just a hinterland of the metropolis.

In the context engaged with by a history of Luddism and the Dark Mountain Project 'countryside' is a space for the supply of goods such as agricultural produce and services such as recreation and leisure to people dwelling within urban or suburban spaces. There is not the stark City-Country division of the popular imagination. This situation is illustrated well by the anthropologist Hugh Brody in his account of the visit to London in 1976 of an indigenous Inuit man called Anaviapik. Brody had spent many years in the area known as the Canadian high arctic engaging in ethnographic research and land rights issues with Inuit communities and state institutions. This visit to London was arranged to facilitate the editing of a film illustrating the culture, livelihoods and land use practices of indigenous arctic communities. The visit presented interesting interactions as it was the first time Anaviapik had left the high arctic. Brody describes how they spent much of their time in London, but he felt the desire to show the visitor some of the English countryside. To this end he chose the most 'rural' route he could think of close to London and headed into East Anglia, through Cambridgeshire, Suffolk and Norfolk;

> "He [Anaviapik] looked out onto the green landscapes and said, "It's all built." He did not see the difference between town and country except as a matter of degree: the one had more people and more houses side by side, and the other had more fields and hedgerows. But all of this, hedgerows as much as houses, was made by people; none of it was "nature" – at least, not a form of nature that he would recognise as such. ... he did not like much of what he saw." (Hugh Brody)[322]

My point in describing urbanism as an issue for the Luddites, and the project under discussion here and to illustrate it with the lengthy passage above, is to demonstrate the complex issues presented by the potential 'collapse' of the first globalised civilisation. WH Auden in making a narrative of the fall of Roman Civilisation concludes his piece with an image of a vast untouched wilderness:

> *Altogether elsewhere, vast*
> *Herds of reindeer move across*
> *Miles and miles of golden moss,*
> *Silently and very fast.*
> (WH Auden)[323]

As things fall apart again there is becoming less and less that is "altogether elsewhere", and this is a key point of significance for 'Uncivilised' art and expression or any critique searching for an 'outside' to modernity. Hardt takes this as a central theme in his "Global Society of Control"[324], and suggests (following Frederic Jameson) that in the post-modern world "there is no more outside"[325]. This in fact is how he defines the transition from 'modern' to 'postmodern'. Just as the "walls of the institutions are breaking down", not as the downfall of disciplinary technique but as its generalization "across the social field"[326], so the "civil order" with its external counterpoint of "nature" theorized by Hobbes and Rousseau has become 'total'. "The process of modernization, then, [...] is the internalization of the outside, that is, the civilization of nature"[327]. As a response to this very situation I would argue that 'Uncivilisation' is a search for the fragments of wildness that can be found in the cracks of the totality. Whether these cracks are permaculture gardens in crumbling post-industrial cities such as Detroit, residents reclaiming a Scottish island from an absentee Laird[328] or the few uncontacted tribes remaining in the Amazon basin dodging and resisting industrial expansion. 'Uncivilisation' is an exploration of what it means to dwell on that which has not been domesticated or which is slipping free of its domestication. By using the term 'cracks' I am deliberately alluding to the Zapatista desire "to open a crack in history"[329] when we are told to accept that "in a postmodern world all phenomena and forces are artificial, or as some might say, part of history" (Hardt)[330].

Having compared the Dark Mountain Project with another 'manifesto' from the 'edge', explored its expression through a 'nomadic' 'minoritarian' history of the Luddites and discussed what it may mean to undo 'progress' by finding the wild cracks within a technological totality I will now explore how collapse invokes a time of 'mourning'. I have already stated that a central point of the Dark Mountain Project is that the current global crisis cannot be reduced to a linear problem-solution reading and that the everyday affective experience of being within this crisis is a starting point for going outside this reductionism. Something that can be taken from the project in this regard is to name a need felt by many for mourning what has been lost and will be lost. This mourning requires a non-anthropocentric approach to relationality. As the manifesto states "Humans are not the point and purpose of the planet. Our art will begin with the attempt to step outside the human bubble. ... we will reengage with the non-human world"[331]. A movement has emerged over recent years to promote a day of remembrance for lost species and this theme has been taken up by some under the 'uncivilisation' umbrella[332], including an art installation and session at the 2013 festival. The point of this is to raise the question of what it feels like to dwell within an 'extinction crisis' (named by some as the 'Anthropocene Extinction Event'[333]) when thousands of species are lost largely unnoticed every year. Kathryn Yusoff, drawing upon the work of Judith Butler, describes how naming the banal violence implicit in a human-oriented social world is to risk a mourning for the loss represented by extinctions. "..., extinction still marks us darkly, because it is lost to relation"[334]. In common with the violence of the frontier, survey, and grid[335] discussed in previous chapters the violence that is invoked here by Yusoff would be baulked at by those used to defining violence in a purely interpersonal anthropocentric sense. Yusoff and others however demand an approach that sees violence as a relational matter within a multiplicity or assemblage that does not mark its boundaries by the limits of the human social world. She emphasises that the world is co-constituted by a vast interrelation of biodiversity. Thus a "loss requires mourning and grieving for the destruction of a relation and those subjects that are constituted through that relation" (Yusoff)[336]. In addition to mourning the loss of species to live at a singularity when things may fall apart is to mourn the loss of the lifestyles that have become normalized to us. To let go of the 'myth of progress' may be easy to describe but in practice devastating in the short term. This myth is largely a superstructure upon which western citizens peg our security, this is how we give an account of the purpose of our daily activities and our plans for the future. If this security is taken away, even if it is pathological and violent to individuals and the biosphere, it will be felt by many as a loss. For example, in a collapsing civilization a career pathway with a funded retirement will become largely meaningless, as will aspiring to a new car or house or any number of goals that make sense to a subjectivity formed within modernity. So to name a need for mourning is a radical step, in that it refuses to reduce this crisis to a technical malfunction in need of a fix and faces head on the full emotional, traumatic and affective implications of the age.

In drawing my schizoanalytic engagement with this case study to a close I wish to emphasise that the Dark Mountain Project is all about stories. While there may be some suspicion of the subjectivity involved in the use of stories to deny their significance is to deny that "knowledge is narratively constructed"[337]. The Dark Mountain Project warns that not only hubris but danger lies in denying the role stories play in constructing our existence.

> "If we are indeed teetering on the edge of a massive change in how we live, in how human society itself is constructed, and in how we relate to the rest of the world, then we were led to this point by the stories we have told ourselves – above all, by the story of civilization" (Kingsnorth and Hine)[338].

The implication, however, is that by engaging with stories and finding new stories there is a possibility of navigating the future.

John Gray[339] may reject 'Uncivilisation', suggesting that cool heads are what is needed at this moment of crisis, but surely a multiplicity of approaches are needed to engage with such a complex moment of dis-ease. Stories may take the form of "small stories" telling the local and particular, they may be "storying (for) change" as a prefigurative action or they may be simply "telling stories" as a way to communicate[340]; there is no hierarchy of these types, just a rhizomatic deployment as a pragmatic practice to see us into and through these times. A new particular story is not being proposed in a fascist authoritarian fashion, just a desire for new stories to seed within the cracks in the old. These cracks may appear on their own or they may be smashed open from within or without, all that matters is that the cracks open to make a space for the wild and undomesticated – the uncivilized.

RADICAL IMPLICATIONS OF A WILD SCHIZOANALYSIS

TENTACLES OF MENTAL DISTRESS AND MODERNITY

"What if all our efforts toward liberation are determined by an ideology which despite our desire for a better world leads us inevitably back to the old paradigm of suffering?" (Susan Griffin)[341]

In this piece of writing I have been out for a walk with the schizophrenic, as Deleuze and Guattari advise[342], instead of remaining indoors with the neurotic on the couch. Remembering and emphasising again that a schizoanalytic walk is not "a goal or an end in itself"[343]. This walk took us through the jungles of Chiapas with a Mayan rebel army, on into the traumatised late modern spaces of indigeneity and resistance in Turtle Island (Canada/USA) and finishing teetering on the edge of a cliff, daring to look over and pondering the collapse of civilisation. The walk is the methodology, to conduct a schizoanalysis is to be on the move, not to attempt to capture a 'freeze-frame' snapshot of time. This is a nomadic methodology that attempts to step into the 'flow', not to study the flow as some distant detached observer, but to be a part of that flow. It is a delusion to believe that research could be truly real, valuable and qualitative without the researcher becoming a part of it, acknowledging our embeddedness, and knowing that we could effect change by being there. So having left my schiz-walk on the cliff edge, wavering as if awaiting a sequel, I will now return to the inquiry that I was hoping to shed some light upon.

The quote at the start of this chapter by Susan Griffin captures succinctly the problematic that I wish to address. My problematic being the experience and proliferation of mental distress in the spaces of modernity. Griffin's quote is significant in that there is indeed generally a desire for liberation and a 'better world' amongst those with an interest in mental distress (or mental health as the issue is optimistically phrased). This includes service users, psy-professionals and health and social care planners. There is no dark conspiracy in play to over-see the continued proliferation, diversification and intensification of mental distress (although I suggest one may suspend this beneficent assumption when considering the actions of pharmaceutical companies!). As she states it is "despite our desire" we are led "back to the old paradigm of suffering". She uses the term 'ideology', which I have tended to avoid for the most part, but it is a serviceable way of describing 'modernity'. At this point I want to bring back the quote from John Zerzan used at the start of my introduction; "To assert that we can be whole/enlightened/healed within the present madness amounts to endorsing the madness"[344]. To juxtapose this with Griffin's words brings some further clarity to the situation. Zerzan is identifying the delusion of aiming for liberation or for a better world without acknowledging the context or totality of the problematic milieu. Again we can see that there is no conspiracy to be uncovered that will suddenly liberate my problematic. The case is far more complex, as the overlapping and intertwined tentacles of modernity and mental distress are very much a part of one organism and cannot be neatly prised apart for dissected analysis. The crux here is that most attempts or techniques developed or proposed to alleviate mental distress are from exactly the same linear 'myth of progress' thinking that is so inseparable from the genesis of the distress in the first place. Hence the intertwining tentacles of modernity and mental distress.

DISCIPLINARY MODERNITY AND CONTROL HYPERMODERNITY

Having reached this point I will draw in the material I have used to define modernity, as it is a multi-faceted term with numerous contested definitions. It will be recalled that I discussed modernity as having associations with more concrete forms such as the industrial revolution as a historical period and the Enlightenment as a revolution in philosophical world-view. The emergence of the scientific technique as rational movement of linear progress was mirrored in social and political thought by figures such as Hegel. He carries the idea of society moving in one direction from a past of disorder to a future fulfilment through the resurrection of the dialectical method of thesis meeting antithesis and correcting in a synthesis. Enlightenment thought, however, does not represent such a radical break with the pre-modern as it could be argued it simply exchanges the metaphysics of an all knowing God for the metaphysics of a rational subject. So "the enlightenment's metaphysical and epistemological assessment of

the world was continuous with pre-modern
thought in so far as it also still seemed to assume
the idea of an ordered whole" (Lumsden)[345].
Alleged continuity with the past aside I have
characterised modernity as being a dis-ease on
both the personal subjective experiential and the
collective and material planes. This character
disrupts an assumed faith in progress that
justifies keeping the cogs in motion. Members of
the Frankfurt School were some of the earlier
thinkers to give modernity's 'dark side' a
sustained analysis. An example of this being
Adorno's "Negative Dialectic" in which the
synthesis produced by the dialectic is anything
but a step towards a future fulfilment. So while
an ordered whole may be strived towards this
'whole' becomes a totalitarian nightmare, not
necessarily the totality of jack boots and
swastikas, but the more subtle totality of the
control society.

This modernity of faith in an ordered whole
is, however, a refrain of life that has grown old.
We find ourselves "at the point of the decay of an
epoch" where the dominant stories have "begun
to lose their explanatory cogency" (Lumsden)[346].
Hence the scramble to adequately theorise the
stage we are at, which some call post-modern,
some hyper-modern, others late-modern and a
host of other terms. Zygmunt Bauman[347]

captures the lack of clarity and shifting sands of the time very visually with his term "liquid modernity". This is also where Deleuze's "control society"[348] emerges as a term of reference, for describing a new phase of organising beyond (but also co-existing with) Foucault's sovereign and disciplinary societies. I have argued that psychiatry found its genesis in the early modern Enlightenment period and has been fixed in lock-step with the twists and turns of the project of modernity ever since. This helps to explain the seeming liberation that many though would be heralded by unlocking hospital ward doors and the scaling back of the large psychiatric institutions in the western world over the past 30 years. I continue to suggest that this has, unsurprisingly, not been a liberation, just a shift mirroring the wider post/late/hyper/liquid modern context. The institution has been totalised across the social field, as John Berger puts it "across the planet we are living in a prison" and all are fellow prisoners, while "penitentiaries still exist and more and more are being built. But prison walls now serve a different purpose. What constitutes an incarceration area has been transformed"[349]. Or as Deleuze expressed in his original societies of control theorising, the "old disciplines operating in the time frame of a closed system" have been and are being replaced by "ultra-rapid forms of free floating control"[350].

In my research I have given modernity a particularly spatial definition, and this is not accidental. The spaces of mental distress, both the discrete spaces of treatment and the wider spaces of everyday modernity, I believe are key to understanding the problem at hand. The 'Societies of Control' thesis is overtly spatial in that it implies a shifting or abolition of boundaries between an inside and an outside. This is both philosophical and knowledge boundaries, but also physical boundaries of walls, fences, locked/unlocked doors and borders. Deleuze ruminates that "new forms of resistance" will be needed in this situation, new theorising, new imagination to envisage an adequate response to the complex "coils of a serpent"[351]. "The man of control is undulatory, in orbit, in a continuous network"[352] this is a slippery adversary in constant motion, one coil appears as enemy, another as friend and yet another appears as a mirror. I am in agreement that new forms of resistance are required, specifically in this case new approaches and explanatory tools to comprehend mental distress. The anti-psychiatry of Laing, Cooper, et al, is no longer up to the task, likewise the critique of Oedipus and Psychoanalysis now seems quaint as mental distress has passed into the hands of bio-medical epistemologies and pharmaceutical marketing. Those earlier critiques were appropriate to the disciplinary modern society but "psychiatry is [now] so heavily bent toward a biomedical understanding of mental illness and so dependent on psychotropic solutions for emotional problems that it might be characterised as not simply modern but rather hypermodern" (Michel)[353].

PREFIGURATION, PRAGMATICS AND DECOLONISATION

So we have reached a point in this critique where psychiatry has been situated as a practice of modernity. Modernity has been problematised as having a dis-ease, not as an aberrant dysfunction but as a core function of its unfolding. Mental distress is a part of this dis-ease and it is interwoven in a complex manner. We have then seen how a myth of liberation has seen psychiatry as one of many social forces that have become 'hypermodern'. Bringing this process to light demands new types of resistance and the point of the rest of this piece will be to suggest appropriate modes of resistance. This will be a two-fold mixture, firstly of prefigurative practices, as I have suggested before this is

'building a new world within the shell of the old'.
Secondly in the mix will be pragmatic practices
that acknowledge that too much 'solutioneering'
is part of the problem in the first place and
resistance will have to be flexible enough to see
cracks open and respond in particular times and
places as things unfold. An insight I drew from
the Dark Mountain Project and from 'The
Coming Insurrection' was that we are currently
living through a "live pragmatics of collapse" and
I aim to hold this in creative tension with an
anarchist prefigurative hope. My two-fold
resistance relies on one major crux of my
critique; the existence of an 'outside' to
modernity. This is the base which makes any
critique not just a nihilist despair but a ready
possibility to be productive. Modernity rests upon
the assumption of its universality: "Nothing at
all may remain outside, because the mere idea of
outsideness is the very source of fear" (Adorno
and Horkheimer)[354]. This is true of utopian
Enlightenment thought in its teleological
process, and it remains true of a late/post/hyper-
modernity with its generalised techniques of
control. As previously stated, these claims to
universality are a "myth of mythlessness"[355] or a
"tradition not aware of itself as a tradition"[356].
Getting a purchase on the chinks in modernity's
armour is reliant upon upsetting this

universalist claim.

> "The awareness of the exteriority of modernity comes hand in hand with the questioning of modernity's universal validity claims and more specifically of the modern/colonial rule over 'the real'" (Vazquez)[357]
> "We need to disobey these methodologies and proceed in a different way" (Vazquez)[358]

The existence of an 'outside' to modernity is a conclusion to be draw from all three of the case studies explored in previous chapters. The Zapatista struggle was in large part an embarrassment to a modernist/modernising Mexican state, the existence of actors who would rather not partake in the building of a 'first world' state was not a role the dominant story had accounted for. This led, in their 'constructivist turn', into getting on and creating different modes of organisation, actively demonstrating that there was more than one way to exist in a space and to construe social relations. To be immersed in this kind of prefiguration is to very soon see modernity as just one story among many. Similarly in my analysis of 'Idle No More', in their refusal of modernist laws, naming schemes and borders in favour of non-Cartesian embodied ways of understanding, we can see a suppressed outside being re-opened and explored. What was particularly interesting here was the trauma and distress involved in many centuries of enforcing a demarcated modern colonial 'inside'. There is insight to be gained from the search for healing of trauma by these indigenous groups, an example being the blockading of problematic 'flows' and the re-opening of healthy flows (flows that ignore borders) to engage with a landscape therapeutically. Finally I characterised 'Uncivilisation' as a "re-wilding from within", with a "keen eye to an 'outside' that hasn't been colonised ... or that is loosening the colonising grip." This project is the search for new stories that can be an insurrection to derail the death ride of progress. What draws all of these expositions of an 'outside' together is a drive to 'de-colonise', that is they are not static critiques but are in 'movement' actively looking to shake off the totalised colonial present. They are not accepting the actual, the dominant version of the 'real', but are searching the 'virtual' for other possibilities and other configurations. They are all engaged in de-colonial practices, if we accept that modernity itself is, as Habermas[359] suggests, a colonisation of the lifeworld. This perspective points towards post-colonial and de-colonial theory and practice as being useful approaches to my pre-figurative and pragmatic resistance to modernity's 'rational management' of mental distress.

I must be cautious at this stage not to be a male European clumsily appropriating de-colonial theory for my own ends. As Walter Mignolo has extensively documented, de-colonial thought and practices date all the way back to the renaissance period of European expansion[360], and not just to a recent "de-colonial turn"[361] noted in academic circles. As with the Zapatista uprising, this is a rage at least 500 years in the making, and significantly a rage against colonialism that is still very much a contemporary problem. Despite the common belief in Europe that the colonial period is past, it has stayed very much present, for example, in the form of 'epistemological colonialism' – a process by which western hierarchies of knowledge are naturalised as the 'only' objective empirical logic[362]. Thus only certain questions come to be seen as relevant or sensible and diverse practices and knowledges are dismissed as 'other'. De-colonialism is well defined as a "scepticism", a "scepticism towards dehumanizing forms of thinking that present themselves as natural or divine-, [this scepticism] animate[s] new forms of theorizing based on the scandal in [the] face of the continuity of dehumanizing practices and ideas" (Maldonato-Torres)[363]. These new forms of theorizing, or "transmodernity" in the words of Enrique Dussel, represent "the horizon of a possible decolonized world"[364]. This is "the transgression and transcendence of modernity, understood as a system premised on colonizing ideas, institutions and practices"[365]. These words are a good summary of the resistance I have suggested will be necessary to formulate an adequate response to mental distress in the spaces of modernity. My pre-figurative and pragmatic resistance will, if it is to have any efficacy at all, be a transgression and a transcendence of modernity.

Remaining cautious of the risk of expropriating ideas in a classically colonial fashion, I should point out that other figures have directly made these connections between the domains of modernity, colonialism, psychiatry and mental distress. Most notable among these figures is arguably Frantz Fanon, a French educated psychiatrist of Algerian descent. Fanon identified the social and political elements of mental distress that he saw while working in Algiers from 1953 until his resignation from his medical post in the colonial administration in

1956 to join the Algerian liberation movement. What is instructive for my use of decolonisation as resistance is Fanon's identification of not just a neutral biological disease pathway in those experiencing mental distress, but the functioning of colonialism on the libidinal and psychic planes. This analysis took him within a matter of years from the hospital to the scene of a violent rupture of colonialism; Just as I am searching outside the hospital for the 'cracks' or 'ruptures' within modernity to get some purchase on an analysis of mental distress. This position acknowledges that it is not enough to simply put 'service users' in already extant positions of power, as this is merely playing around with the roles in an already present colonial game. More than this game is needed, as Samira Kawash situates this Fanonian 'rupture'; "true decolonization is something much more radical than the reversal of position and the replacement of rulers; decolonization is the uprooting of the system as a whole, the supplanting of the political, existential, and corporeal reality created by colonization"[366]. She also suggests that Fanon's analysis doesn't take a Hegelian view of 'progress' but something more akin to Walter Benjamin's redemptive dialectic of revolution; this is the position that the moment we find ourselves in and the possibilities therein are not reduced to a point on a one way line of 'progress' or historical teleology, but that this moment can "blast open the continuum of history" (Benjamin)[367]. This is thus the fear that the Algerian resistance struck into the French colonial psyche and also the fear that a resistance to modernity strikes into those invested in the project of progress; "the "terror" of decolonization is the terror of radical possibility generated from within the scene of colonization" (Kawash)[368].

ABSTRACT SPACE: ABSTRACT DISTRESS

The scene of de/colonisation within which I am seeking a Fanonian rupture is the abstract space of modernity. Within such an abstract space mental distress has become and can only be seen as an ahistorical abstraction. The meaning of such an assertion will become clear if we explore theorisations of abstract space further. Mick Smith elaborates this concept of 'abstract space' by drawing upon Le Corbusier's modernist writings on city planning. He suggests that "modernity's principle is repetition" and that its modus operandi is the "creation of types and through the eradication of difference"[369]. Le Corbusier champions this principle by demanding "the erasure of the specificity of both past and place. [...] to break free from both the 'slime' of social history and the unwelcome intrusions of nature's 'disorderly' conduct"[370]. I am arguing that Le Corbusier's modernist dream of city planning echoes exactly the dream of modern psychiatry. The overt aim of so called "evidence based" psychiatry is the establishment of 'objective' universal standards, diagnostics and interventions that can shake off the weight of the checkered history of approaches to mental distress. This aim is to "build on a clear site [...] to replace the 'accidental' lay-out of the ground" (Le Corbusier)[371]. The modern city and the modern technique of 'health' thus become one and the same thing, they are the embodiment of the intertwining tentacles discussed previously. Thus "the nature and origins of our distress remain hidden from us, and it becomes 'free floating', unanchored to any recognisable 'cause'" (Kidner)[372], just as the interior of our mass produced car, office with its suspended ceilings and plastic carpet or brick box in suburbia are shy at disclosing their origins, are 'free floating' and literally 'could be anywhere'. David Kidner analyses this abstraction in the case of 'depression', arguing that the industrial domain comes to re-define 'human welfare' thereby 'misconstruing human needs' as an unacknowledged emergent property of the normal functioning of industrial society[373]. Thus he concludes that as the 'natural' world of a healthy bio-diverse environment is systematically impoverished and destroyed, so is the human psyche in exactly the same fashion. The crux of this matter is, however, that a 'firewall' is built between the two domains thus obscuring their virtually identical unfolding, leaving depression, anxiety and the like as individual problems, "reflecting personal inadequacy" and demanding individualised solutions/treatments[374].

In this setting mental distress becomes a matter of the individual and a universal individual at that. The 'gold standard' of psychiatric classifications such as the ICD-10 (WHO 1992) or symptom/treatment rating scores such as the Health of the Nation Outcome Score (HoNOS) or Montreal Cognitive Assessment (MoCA) is that they could be applicable to a person anywhere on the globe, despite the European and North American origins of these classifications[375]. The ICD-10 manual gives each disorder a numeric code that is then able to be integrated into digital record keeping systems. Even though there are many hundreds of such codes within the manuals, there are many millions of people experiencing mental distress and inevitably these individual embodied subjectivities existing in particular places, spaces and times will have their experience reified into a 'type' that allows limited room for 'difference'. This abstraction of mental distress also demands the presence of professional divisions of labour and these disciplinary divisions then come to define what is understood as mental illness and the appropriate ways of approaching such a condition. John Zerzan has discussed division of labour at length as a disabling development of the civilising process. He suggests, using anthropological and archaeological evidence, that as specialisation of tasks becomes more subdivided and these subdivisions in turn become rigid that a generalised de-skilling occurs along with a loss of wholeness and embeddedness from human experience. Furthermore in this process inter-personal empathy in social relations is no longer innate[376]. He invokes Jacques Ellul as a succinct and visual summary of this problem; "the sharp knife of specialization has passed like a razor into the living flesh"[377]. Badiou suggests that division of labour is a major stumbling block to thinking,

> "the world is essentially a specialized and fragmentary world; fragmented in response to the demands of the

innumerable ramifications of the technical
configuration of things, of the apparatuses
of production, of the distribution of
salaries, of the diversity of functions and
skills. And the requirements of this
specialization and this fragmentation
make it difficult to perceive what might be
transversal or universal;" (Alain Badiou)[378]

Thus with the emergence of a range of psy-
professions in the past 100 years the issue of
mental distress has become reified and reduced.
The use of numeric coding discussed above is a
prime example of this process of capture and
reduction. To be effective, however, in helping
someone in distress often demands resisting this
reification and capture. The psychotherapist
Nick Totton criticises the regulatory professional
culture as being bound up with the processes of
domestication of the wild discussed in previous
chapters. He suggests that therapeutic helping
practices are "impossible to domesticate without
disempowering [...]: therapy is, in fact,
inherently wild, and cannot be rendered safe in
the way that regulation processes intend"[379].
Thus, despite the fact that professional
regulation may indeed 'protect' the pubic in a
mass culture and in a one-dimensional fashion,
there is a whole world of richness and diversity

in skills of helping distress that is lost in the process.

So, returning to my characterisation of 'abstract distress' within 'abstract spaces', I hope that some clarity has been provided as to the nature of what is distinct and problematic about mental distress in the spaces of modernity. As a final illustration and to carry the discussion forward I would like to again cross the 'firewall' mentioned above. Transversal crossing of boundaries being a place where Zerzan and Guattari find a meeting place. This time enclosure of the commons is my image. To make abstract space, commons open to all for all manner of 'wild' practices have to be domesticated, bounded and enclosed. Just as this happened physically in the modern age, as space became exchangeable 'property', with fences, walls, monetary/numeric value and the like, so this happened in the modern psyche. As seen in the example of First Nations communities in Canada and elsewhere, this very process involved trauma: the creation of distress. But it didn't stop with the creation of distress, it then 'captured' this distress, in the 'enclosure' of the psy-commons[380]. Self and communal understandings of distress and how to react to such states were thus denigrated and commodified into the realm of 'experts' and professionals who came to hold a 'monopoly on distress'.

SUBVERSION 1: SCALING UP THE DIAGNOSIS

The first tactic of resistance that I will offer as a response to this individualising and de-skilling enclosure is the appropriation of the diagnostic codes and their re-application at a different and unintended scale. This is an appropriation of the weapons of colonisation, their modification and redeployment as tools of de-colonisation. Gary Genosko illustrates his discussion of Guattari's 'smooth and striated' with just such a re-deployment of tools of oppression. One of the cases he applies is the use, until 1967, of 'disc numbers', 'E numbers' or tags on individual Inuit persons in Yukon and Northwest Territories of Canada to identify them. This numbering system was later replaced by a 'census' requiring individuals to select a recognisable European style name. Both names and numbers were re-deployed in multiple ways, often an individual using a complex combination of names, nicknames, numbers and so forth to describe themselves. Also the discs themselves were physically used as decoration, to identify houses lacking street numbers, on snow-mobiles, in works of art, etc. In one particular instance in 1991 a symbolic numbering system was started by the issuing of 'mock disks' with 'Q' numbers applied to 'Qallunaat' – white people[381]. These examples are the 'escape' of codes from bureaucratic 'overcoding' techniques repeatedly applied as part of the violence of colonialism. In terms of the smooth and the striated Genosko suggests that state bureaucrats will attempt to apply the striations of organisation to indigenous communities; but "there is something smooth about Inuit life that keeps issuing challenges to the self-appointed bestowers of names and number crunchers in state bureaucracies and elsewhere (churches, mining companies, etc)" (Genosko)[382].

My resistance of re-appropriation takes the diagnostic manuals and their numbered codes as medico-legal-bureaucratic striations applied to individuals. In my cases the escape of the code is its application not to individuals but whole societies and institutions. The first example of this is Chellis Glendinning's book "My Name is Chellis and I'm in Recovery from Western Civilization"[383]. Glendinning, a psychotherapist, takes the diagnosis of post-traumatic stress disorder (PTSD) and suggests that it represents the 'normal' state of societal functioning in civilisation.

"...the traumatized state is not merely the domain of the Vietnam veteran or the survivor of childhood abuse; it is the underlying condition of the domesticated psyche" (Glendinning)[384].

She methodically goes through the diagnostic criteria and symptoms demonstrating that they are applicable on a society-wide scale and at this scale are seen not as pathologies but as a typical way to go about everyday life. For example the recurrent intrusive recollections of trauma common to individual PTSD are displayed in the frequent themes of violence, horror and terror in mass entertainment such as films[385]. Another symptom is the numbing of affect, which Glendinning suggests is akin to a "'dead to the world' approach to life [that] has become the modus operandi of most people living in mass technological society... caught in rush-hour traffic, watching television, glued to [the] computer screen... the crowd of paralyzed people in the elevator"[386]. Another symptom, arrested psychosocial development, playing out as widespread infantile approaches to relationships in adults and governments conducting knee-jerk military operations as acts of "revenge"[387]. A final, and pertinent to my argument, symptom

she describes is addictions, particularly the
largely un-questioned techno-addiction which is
the assumed position of 'progress' and growth
economics[388]. Paul Virilio's work touches on some
of these themes. In his "The Original Accident"
he describes the "havoc wreaked by progress" as
the "integral accident" of modernity[389]. In this
analysis he scales-up suicide; this final act has
ceased to be a matter simply of psychology,
"associated with the mentality of a few disturbed
individuals, but sociological and political"[390]. As
stated previously, these societal scale symptoms
are mostly either denied, not analysed or are
naturalised as simply a part of 'human nature'.
The strength of Glendinning's position is that
these symptoms cannot be ignored in such a
fashion, they stand as an indictment of a
pathological modernity that is every bit as
'mentally ill' as the individuals inhabiting it and
to whom diagnostic codes are applied.

The second diagnostic re-appropriation to be
raised here is the book "The Corporation" by Joel
Bakan, the material of which also became the
topic of a documentary film by the same name.
The diagnosis to be used in this case is
Psychopathy and rather than a society wide
application, here the 'patient' is an institution:
The Corporation. Bakan's methodological
application of the DSM IV and ICD-10 criteria

bring him to the conclusion that modern corporations can accurately be described as 'psychopaths'. So while individuals within corporations may present with psychopathic traits in their working practices, they "compartmentalise" these traits[391] and behave differently in their personal lives. The corporation itself, however, is a psychopath through and through, meeting the diagnostic criteria comfortably. Thus "the corporation is singularly self-interested and unable to feel genuine concern for others in any context"[392]. It is "grandiose" in its thinking and planning and is "manipulative" to achieve these ends. It lacks "empathy", is incapable of feeling "remorse", refuses to "accept responsibility" and relates to others "superficially"[393]. The significance of applying this diagnostic formula to a corporation is that in many legal situations these institutions claim the rights of individuals. Thus it seems particularly appropriate to turn the matter around and apply an ICD-10 code that would often lead to the curtailment or restriction of the rights of individuals if they presented with such a pure form of psychopathy and behaved in the same manner. When something usually reductionist and restricting is re-applied in this fashion it shows starkly the farce that the individualising process of categorising distress is, along with the structures of hegemony and power (such as corporations) that maintain and legitimise this process. Similar factors can be seen to come into play with Glendinning's 'socialising' of PTSD; so it is not just individuals alone fighting their intrusive recollections of trauma, but the entire 'civis' together struggling to forget their collective trauma. In some cases this approach could point towards therapeutic practices genuinely helpful to the distressed individual. An example of this is a recent 'novella' "Liminal", written by Natasha Alvarez. Her writing is a journal of a year of 'mourning' that she chose to take in response to her overwhelming feelings. She describes "wrestling with a deep and painful sadness" after the birth of her son[394]. She responded with a widening of the issue, captured beautifully in a brief passage:

> ""Post partum" people said. "Grief," I replied, "mourning for a collapsing ecosystem and a dying planet."" (Alvarez)[395].

This resistance of re-appropriation is transversal in that it crosses the intended boundaries of application of the diagnostic codes. It crosses the artificial divide between the monadic individual subject and the social practices and institutions of which they are a part. In this way it highlights "the erroneousness of dividing the Real into a number of discrete domains" (Guattari)[396]. This re-appropriation is an example of schizoanalysis as a "radical materialist psychiatry" (not just another 'technique' to dwell within the 'psy' domain) and it begins to get some leverage on my problematic of mental distress in the spaces of modernity.

OVERTLY SPATIAL DISTRESS: OR TRAVERSING THE FIREWALL

"What has congealed as an environment is a relationship to the world based on management, which is to say, on estrangement. A relationship to the world wherein we're not made up just as much of the rustling trees, the smell of frying oil in the building, running water, the hubbub of schoolrooms, the mugginess of summer evenings. A relationship to the world where there is me and then my environment, surrounding me but never constituting me. We have become neighbours in a planetary board meeting. It's difficult to imagine a more complete hell." (The Invisible Committee)[397].

Using The Invisible Committee's description of a 'complete hell' in contemporary France as a starting spring board I intend now to carry a line of flight over (or through) the fire wall discussed above. 'Distress' within this 'complete hell' is not 'abstract' distress, neither is space an abstraction in this process. In the place of the desire to see distress as a-historical, a-social and a-spatial my transversal movement will place distress as overtly spatial, specific, relational and embodied. Let me take a detour into archaeology to illustrate this point further and to find another spatial "hell".

In his narrative description of the finds from numerous archaeological digs around the eastern Mediterranean, Steven Mithen characterises the creation of an everyday living 'hell'. The site he particularly describes thus is a Neolithic village dating from 9000-7000BC called Catalhoyuk, in present day Turkey, near the Syrian border. In these early sites of domestication (a problem discussed previously) we see the kinds of spaces both facilitated and necessitated by the technology/technique of sedentary agriculture. Displays of human skulls and Images of animals were found here that suggested a fear of nature and systemised rituals, the 'wild' as something external and a felt need to secure their community from incursion. These images were within an architecture of little variation, with repeated designs and rigidly demarcated areas for specialised activity; "different types of people − old and young, male and female, specialist toolmakers and those without skills − were very restricted as to where they could sit and work within each room. To me it seems as if every aspect of their lives had become ritualised, any independence of thought and behaviour crushed out of them by an oppressive ideology manifest in the bulls, breasts, skulls and vultures. This sounds like living in a Neolithic hell," (Mithen)[398]. This 'hell' is in sharp contrast to the 'heaven' of pre-domesticated hunter-gatherer life from 20,000BC to 11,000BC for which he found evidence from other archaeological investigations.

This experience of taking up settled farming has surprisingly strong resonances with the spatial relationships produced (or exacerbated) by hyper-modernity; if we remember the "complete hell" of having become "neighbours in a planetary board meeting" (The Invisible Committee)[399]. Just as the first farmers had re-situated the 'wild' as separate and external, we 'moderns' now find ourselves as "me and then my environment, surrounding me but never constituting me". The "bulls, breasts, skulls and vultures"[400] may have been replaced with smart phone adverts, plastic wrapped factory chickens and badger culls, but the message is much the same. These are two concrete examples, in the 21st Century and in 7,500BC, of Glendinning's societal PTSD. We find ourselves trapped together in an everyday that is colonised by dysfunctional practices that stem from trauma and are re-producing the trauma. Marcuse calls these practices "enslaving contentment", the daily activities that are little more than "performances required to sustain destructive prosperity"[401]. Awaking daily to participate in routines so familiar and numbing that they are barely even recognised as questions in need of examination, let alone as practices that are built upon resource depletion, slavery (wage and forced) and species extinction. This is the 'uneven' ground that Le Corbusier would like to erase from the equation, there can be no 'commons' for sustenance here, only techniques developed by professionals. The straight and even lines must be built to enable the smooth continuance of 'progress', citizens must forget the uneven ground hidden under and repressive practices hidden by the level concrete floor. If you feel distress in this space it must be a technical problem of biology, chemicals or genes requiring an empirical solution that can be manufactured and reproduced wherever the concrete floor stretches. However, concrete isn't yet everywhere and where it is it has a habit of cracking, and these edges and cracks are where we could begin to situate what Guattari calls "aesthetic-existential"[402] approaches that refuse to "objectify, reify [or] 'scientifise' subjectivity." "It is from such a rupture that an existential singularisation correlative to the genesis of new coefficients of freedom will become possible" (Guattari)[403].

Our task then in drawing this schizoanalysis to a close and to suggest resistances is to make these "new coefficients of freedom" possible. Rather than spatial practices of standardisation and banal repression a possibility of 'anarchic space' can be opened up. Within anarcho-space there is a need to address the inherited distress, as the trauma won't just disappear, thus pragmatic practices can be explored drawing upon a hotch-potch of re-directed existing approaches and what is left of the richness of the psy-commons. There will also be pre-figurative practices that envisage an existence that isn't stuck in constant re-producing trauma. These practices are akin to health promotion, remembering the cliché that 'prevention is better than cure'. To make an illustration of what is required let us consider factory farming as a problem of modernity. This issue can be subdivided into particulars, such as routine over-use of antibiotics. Thus one could campaign against this use of antibiotics, demanding that the practice is stopped. This would, however, ignore the 'assemblage' of factors that make the factory farm what it is. The antibiotic use is necessitated by the crowded conditions and the vectors and mutations of disease in such a space. The crowded space is necessitated by the imperative to maximise profit with the highest yields possible in the area available. This argument goes on through multiple levels of organisation, philosophical and material considerations, and in a complex non-linear causative fashion. Through this we find that factory farming is another 'technique' that is hyper-modern through and through. Thus to effectively challenge the problem of factory farming one would need to take an 'assemblage' view and not just look at one single issue. This methodological insight remains true in an assessment of mental distress. One could demand the cessation of the use of psychotropic medication, but fail to address the reasons that the use of such medication has become the accepted way to approach mental distress. It would also risk stigmatising people who find such substances genuinely helpful in managing day to day. Thus I want to suggest that pre-figurative resistances to create anarcho-space and the pragmatic approaches also will need to be such 'assemblage' views. This is why a richly spatial approach is helpful – by refusing to see distress as 'free-floating' and abstract and thus requiring interventions that are every bit as reductionist, we can see the fire wall that we plan to traverse. To achieve such a goal and as a finale to this chapter and my investigation I shall now appraise the interventions, tools and skills at hand.

SUBVERSION 2: LUDDITE HEALTH PROMOTION

Preventing distress and helping someone who is in distress are tasks requiring skill. I want to suggest, using an argument developed in anthropology by Tim Ingold, that what currently passes for 'health promotion' and 'helping' in situations of mental distress is closer to de-skilling machine operation. Ingold dismisses the traditional idea of technology evolving on a linear trajectory from simple to complex and thus seeing 'primitive' societies as possessing less technical know-how and awaiting development. His suggestion is that it is in fact a matter of the subject being "drawn from the centre to the periphery of the labour process"[404]. The belief that technology is a matter of machines and that these are external to society is a recent one, born of the transition to the 'modern' world wrought by Enlightenment and industrialism. This move to the periphery turns the "workman" into "an *operative*, putting into effect a set of mechanical principles that are both embedded in the construction of the instruments he uses, and entirely indifferent to his own subjective aptitudes and sensibilities"[405]. In this way the operative is "detached from" the process and end product. Ingold calls the opposite approach "technique" (not in the sense that Jacques Ellul uses this term), this way is at the "centre" and "immanent", seeking to minimise the distance between the subject and the process. In this approach the tool is inert until the skilled subject "delivers a force that is personal rather than mechanical"[406], there is no pre-given or independent instrumental objective embedded in this type of tool. Rather the 'process' is embedded in social relations. To use such a tool is to be highly skilled, overturning the old notion of the 'primitive', this skill being "at once a form of knowledge and a form of practice"[407]. Thus "acting in the world is the skilled practitioner's way of knowing it"[408].

Having defined Ingold's use of the term 'technology' and' technique' let me return to my earlier assertion about current interventions for those in distress. I would argue that most 'psy' professions, guided by notions of 'evidence based practice', are more akin to the 'operatives' on the periphery of the process using machines with pre-determined functions. This situation has been an emergent property of the push to standardise interventions coupled with the drive by different 'expert' groupings to professionalise their domain. Thus recalling my discussion of Susan Griffin's essay on ideology it seems that "despite our desire"[409] well intentioned professionals find they are wielding machines over which they have little agency. These machines are of numerous forms, for example mental health legislation is just such a machine, as are prescription guidelines, pharmaceutical formulations, assessment protocols, Cognitive Behavioural Therapy (CBT) sessions, shift working patterns and the built environment of wards and clinics. So if this striated space of abstract universal interventions represents an undesirable mass factory of psy labour, how can we pre-figure an anarcho-space of immanent skilled technique (Ingold's meaning of 'technique'). How can the bored operative putting in a shift at the psy-factory be replaced by the alert, engaged and nuanced hunter-gatherer of the psyche moving with skill in a smooth space?

In answer to this I will suggest another subversive practice: Luddite health promotion. The Luddite actions of the early industrial period were discussed previously in the context of the Dark Mountain Project, and here I will briefly revisit some of the issues raised. The Luddites of the nineteenth century English midlands were generally skilled crafts people, concerned about the dramatic changes they saw coming from the implementation of standardised machine operations in their industries[410]. This situation sits comfortably within Ingold's characterisation of technology with the 'operative' on the 'periphery'. While the Luddites were far from pre-civilised skilled tool users, they were on this trajectory from tool use by skilled subjects in the 'centre' towards an alienated 'periphery'. Their response was "violent in its rhetoric and as direct as a sledgehammer in its actions" (Jones)[411]. For a core period of three years numerous autonomous groups donned masks and smashed the machines responsible for the deterritorialisation of their daily life. While being cautious not to simplify or distort historical events from 200 years ago[412] it seems that to negotiate and accommodate became unthinkable for many in a situation that was driving thousands in the midlands and north of England into poverty and drudgery[413].

Returning to the alienation and limited efficacy of machine interventions in the psy-factory (remaining cautious of clumsily appropriating a 200 year old movement, as neo-luddites have been accused of[414]) I want to open up a space where these type of questions of technology may be asked. This could be in dialogue, in epistemological questions, or equally it could be in visceral direct actions. The question of flows could be re-visited here, as it has been a topic emerging at numerous points in my investigation. Deleuze and Guattari examined the flows of desire, the decoded capitalist flows and the schizophrenic flows. The Zapatistas created their own autonomous flows, whilst ignoring or fighting the statist and neo-colonial flows of capital, commodities and rancher/paramilitary thugs. Idle No More saw blockaded flows to disrupt the violent economy of extraction, trauma and cultural genocide. The Invisible Committee discuss the urban-suburban-exurban flows that maintain the 'nightmare' of modernity and advocate action to disrupt these flows. The Anthropocene has recently been defined partly by the initiation of flows, the global exchange of species that is now imprinted on the geological record[415]. The myth of progress is the engine that drives the flows of destruction along their linear track and surely a subversive practice of Luddite Health Promotion should look to derail this train. There are echoes of this in the derailment of a coal train in the Mace Creek region of northwest Missouri in June 2015. In this action anonymous anarchists became part of an assemblage as they joined forces with heavy rain to weaken vulnerable sections of the line over a number of weeks. Their statement sums up an attitude of transversal movement across domains of psychological health, physical health and ecological health:

> "We do this in solidarity with all prisoners and in defense of the stolen resources of this planet used to kill us. We do this for those made sick and dead and full of cancers by the forces of capitalism. When we do this we mean we have decided not to die." (Earth First Journal)[416]

The nature of the questions and the situation of hyper-modernity that we find ourselves in will determine the level of questioning required. As with any health promotion the benefits may not be immediately apparent and there may well be some up-front costs. But with an eye to the long game and the pre-figuration of something different there could be our sanity to (re-)gain.

POSTSCRIPT: WANDERING AMONG RUINS

Wherever I have been... rows of chairs, round the walls, round the tables, round the demarcated areas......... school, psych ward, office, nursing home, prison?

Names listed, numbered, checked, grouped.....defined.

Doors locked, sealed, checked, secure.....confined.

Behaviour noted, judged, reduced, boxed, forced...... suppressed.

Hierarchy – (overt and covert) – pressing in, enclosing, watching, noting.....suffocated.

Time linear, rigid, straight, counted...... divided.

Tick tock, tick tock, tick tock.....the hours, the unending hours..... tick tock, tick tock, tick tock..... mind is drifting, somewhere, anywhere...

refocus.... tick tock, tick tock, tick tock, tick tock.... mind drifts.... a glimpse of Eden, a wholeness, a bigger picture..... snapped out of that..... tick tock, tick tock, tick tock...

A barrier erected, another enclosure, physical / psychological / spiritual. My specialisation has been my definition, my modus vivendi, it has kept me, separated me, it has been my meaning – my school, psych ward, office, nursing home, prison.

This is the climate change of the mind. Devastation leads to yet more devastation. Tipping points appear to loom up ahead. Another head filled with dichotomized thinking, barely able to comprehend my own species (let alone an intricate web of life). Distress becomes something to be deflected.... washed in clichés..... Grow up, try to fit in, this is for your safety.

That glimpse of Eden, that lost wholeness.... it keeps coming back. Forced away by conformity. Snapped out of. But it keeps coming back.

This myth of Eden, it is strong and often it feels stronger than its brother, the myth of progress with which I have been told I must participate. Those Mesolithic footprints stretching across the mud on the banks of the Severn, they resonate, beyond logic and into the visceral experience of emotion. There are more, footprints that will never be found. Think of Dogger Land, now just a refrain "Dogger bank" for the sake of ships and the weather they will meet.

This land lost to rising seas would be walk able from my birthplace on the only hill in a flat land. The never to be found footprints. It probably would have been walked, not so many generations ago, by the wanderers who shifted with the seasons. From high to low, along rivers, through woods... but not over stiles or through gates.

Even fewer generations ago people sailed over flooded Dogger Land from their shoreline, looking for freedom, to a "new" land, to join a "new" genocide when faced with some more wanderers who shifted with the seasons, from high to low, along rivers, through woods... but not over stiles or through gates.

Inundations from the sea, arrivals of agriculture, languages lost, fences erected, fleeing to the "new" world to found a sprawling city of a familiar name. Collapse has visited my birthplace before. The shape of streets and buildings seen in the turf at Gainsthorpe. Walking distance from the hill in the flat land. Collapse here had come as disease born of domesticates and carried west on trade routes. Plague.

I have been carried west of the hill in the flat land. Carried in that post-modern rootless way, a mixture of ego, hubris and anxiety. Continuing the westward flow from the wreckage of the Fertile Crescent. Not as far as the Mayflower, but still west. There is a more immediate resonance in this place west, amidst an old language of the Britons. Wanderers can be felt in that visceral way on the heights of Plynlimon and Cefn Bryn. The red "lady" of Paviland is close and watches over his broad plain to Exmoor. The footprints stretch into the mud...

Kindred, however, is east. Drawn on walls at Creswell Crags, wandering through post-glacial woods. Before the fences, seeds and hierarchies arrived from the Fertile Crescent. Before coal was torn from this ground and industry left its wreckage as it retreated to find "new" lands. Other things resonate as my kindred in the east, near the only hill in a flat land. The myth-history of Sherwood can be visceral on a misty autumn day lost amidst the oaks, with only a bike for company. Wanderers again, this time seeking refuge from a king or a baron or a law.

Maybe it was the hands of my kin that decorated those Creswell walls and wandered and left footprints and knew the seasons. Wandering from high to low, along rivers, through woods...

Collapse visited as it will visit my life, and maybe then I will wander not so far from the land of my birth.....with the wreckage all around.

ENDNOTES

1. Zerzan 2002, p 158
2. Pilgrim 2007, p. 536
3. Lewis 2006, p 61
4. Bauman 2000
5. Zerzan 2012
6. Giddens 1990
7. Guattari 2013 [1989], pp 6-11
8. Delanty 1999
9. Giddens 1991
10. Griffiths 2000
11. Virilio 2008 [1995], p 58
12. Virilio 2007 [2005], p 19
13. Bauman 2008, p110-111
14. Adorno and Horkheimer 1997 [1944], p 24
15. Ibid, p 3
16. Freud 2004 [1930]
17. eg. Horkheimer 2012 [1974]
18. Virilio 2002, pp 12-13
19. eg, Alexander 2013
20. Holbrook-Pierson 2006
21. Lefebvre 1991
22. eg. Lovelock 2006; Monbiot 2007; Hansen 2011
23. eg. Klein 2000; Stiglitz 2003
24. Lyotard 1984
25. Giddens 1990
26. Bauman 2000

27. Bauman 2000

28. Virilio 2008

29. Hardt 1998a

30. Foucault 1991 [1975]

31. Deleuze 1992

32. Vetter 2012, p 59

33. Bracken, P, Thomas, P, et al. 2012

34. Deleuze and Guattari 2013 [1980]

35. Holmes, Gastaldo and Perron 2007

36. Guattari 2013 [1989], p 19

37. Giddens 1990

38. Lefebvre 1991, pp 367-368, following Foucault 2002 [1969]

39. Deleuze and Guattari 2009 [1972]

40. Deleuze and Guattari 2013 [1980]

41. Dosse in Guattari 2009a,pp 8-11

42. Buchanan 2008, p 8

43. Deleuze and Guattari 2009 [1972], p 296

44. Guattari 2009a

45. Deleuze and Guattari 2009 [1972], p 29

46. Fox 1995, p 78

47. Holland 2013, p 113

48. Guattari 2009b, pp 21-32

49. Ibid, p 21

50. Brown and Tucker 2010, p 229

51. Genosko 2009, ff 134-

52. Deleuze and Guattari 2013 [1980], pp 420-436

53. Ibid, p 122

54. Ibid, ff 409

55. Ibid, p 421

56. Holmes, Gestaldo and Perron 2007

57. Guattari 2009a, p 193

58. Ibid, p 182

59. Smith 2001a, pp 131-149
60. eg. Hidaka 2012
61. Gonzalez 2010, p 3
62. Ibid, p 8
63. Ince 2012
64. Ibid, p 1646
65. Smith 2001b
66. Ibid, p 32
67. Ibid, p 33
68. Blomley 2003
69. Ibid, pp 123-125
70. Ibid, p 130
71. Ibid, p 130
72. Smith 2001b, p 34
73. Ibid, p 33
74. Ibid, p 35
75. Blomley 2003
76. Smith 2001a, p 203
77. Debord 1955, p 26
78. Blomley 2003, p 130
79. Zerzan 2008, p 78
80. Deleuze and Guattari 2013 [1980], pp 409-492
81. Zerzan 2008, p 60
82. Freud 2004 [1930]
83. Zerzan 2008, p 60
84. Levi-Strauss 2013 [1978], pp 11-19
85. Zerzan 2008, pp 80-81
86. Ellul 1964 [1954]
87. Mumford 2010 [1934]
88. Karim 2001, p 118
89. Becker 2010. Lucas and Barrett 1995
90. Smith 2007, p 480
91. Midgley 2003, pp 13-20

92. Smith 2007, p 482

93. Anderson 1997

94. Ibid, p 477

95. Diamond, 1998; Mithen, 2004; Becker 2010

96. Mithen, 2004, p 504

97. Becker 2010, p 12

98. Blomley 2003

99. Anderson 1997, p 491

100. Anderson 1997

101. Griffin 1994 [1978]

102. Castree 2005, p 187-191

103. Holmes, Murray, Perron and Rail 2006

104. Ibid, p 181

105. Illich 1977 [1975]

106. Ibid, p 129

107. Conrad 2007, p 149

108. Ellul 1964 [1954]

109. Peacock and Nolan 2000, p 1069

110. Leboyer 1987 [1974]

111. eg Oakley 1980

112. Crossley 2006, p 48

113. Foucault in Rabinow (ed) 1991 [1984], pp 124-140

114. Giddens 1991, pp 159-160. Crossley 2006, p 48-49

115. Crossley 2006, pp 277-295

116. Clarke 2003, p 11

117. Williams 2002

118. Johnstone 2008, p 9

119. Sadler 2005

120. Johnstone 2008, p 7

121. eg, Szasz 1974. Coppock and Hopton 2001, pp 80-81

122. Buchanan-Barker and Barker 2009, p 94

123. Hopton 1997. Whitehill 2003

124. Crossley 1998. pp 879-880

125. Crossley 1998. Crossley 2006. pp 99-125

126. eg. Szasz 2009

127. Coppock and Hopton 2001, p 79

128. Ibid, p 80

129. eg Bracken and Thomas 2005

130. Davies, Hoggart and Lees 2002, p 35

131. Silverman 2013, p 351

132. McLuhan 2003 [1964]

133. Davies, Hoggart and Lees 2002, p 34

134. Santos, Nunes and Meneses 2008. Smith 1999

135. Hughes, J, quoted in Davies, Hoggart and Lees 2002, p 35

136. Besley 2013, pp 227-228

137. Guattari 2009b, pp 291-300. Guattari in Genosko 1996, p 116

138. Anderson and Smith 2001, p 7

139. Ibid, p 9

140. eg. Thrift 2007. Anderson and Harrison 2010. Pink 2012

141. Pink 2012, ff 30

142. Habermas 1989 [1981]

143. Koopman 2013, p 156

144. Thrift 2007, p 19

145. Vaneigem 2012 [1967], p 122

146. Deleuze and Guattari 2009 [1972]

147. Foucault, M. in Deleuze and Guattari 2009 [1972], p xiii

148. Deleuze and Guattari 2009 [1972], p 22

149. Polack 2011, p 65

150. Seem, M. in Deleuze and Guattari 2009 [1972], p xxi

151. Roberts 2007, p 119-126

152. Deleuze and Guattari quoted in Roberts 2007, p 126

153. Sauvagnargues 2011, p 176

154. Ibid, p 172

155. Holland 1999, pp 1-24

156. Brown and Tucker, 2010, p 232

157. Holland 2013, p 8

158. Deleuze and Guattari 2013 [1980]

159. Ibid, pp 409-492

160. Ibid, pp 1-27

161. eg. Guattari 2011 [1979]

162. Guattari 2009b, p 205

163. Ibid, 2009b, p 215

164. Bennett 2005, p 445

165. Guattari 1995 [1992], p 35

166. Polack 2011, p 58

167. Sauvagnargues 2011, p 174. Genosko, in Guattari 2008 [1989], pp 57-58

168. Genosko 2009, pp 29-30. Polack 2011, pp 59-60. Guattari 2009a, p 179

169. Glendinning 2007 [1994], p 69

170. Ibid, pp 70-71

171. Ibid, p 71

172. Lefebvre 1991

173. Auge 2009 [1995]

174. Zerzan 2008, pp 3-10. Zerzan 2002, pp 1-16

175. Zerzan 2002, p 2

176. Kidner 2012a. Kidner 2012b

177. Kidner 2012a. Kidner 2012b

178. Smith 2001a, p 203

179. eg. Castree 2005

180. Kidner 2012a. 2007

181. Smith 2001a

182. Ince 2012, p 1652

183. eg. Simonsen 2007

184. Springer 2014a. Springer 2014b. Ince 2012

185. Adorno and Horkheimer 1997 [1944], p 16

186. Simonsen 2007, p 176

187. Conant 2010, p 49.

188. Marcos/Ponce de Lyon 2001, p 13

189. eg. Ronfeldt 1998

190. Nail 2012, pp 142-143

191. Marcos 2006

192. Nail p 28

193. Marcos 2007, pp 22-23

194. eg. Marcos and Ignacio Taibo II 2007 [2005] and Marcos 2003 [1996]

195. eg. Conant 2010, pp 254-255. Higgins 2004, p 186.Carrigan 2001

196. Nail 2012, Conant 2010, Tormey 2006, Holloway 1998

197. Marcos/Ponce de Lyon 2001, p 276

198. Tormey 2006

199. Nail 2010 and 2012

200. Henck 2007

201. Brand and Hirsch 2004

202. Ibid, p 382

203. Ibid, p 374

204. Higgins 2004, p2

205. Niezen 2003

206. Ibid, p 3

207. Ibid, p 5

208. Bodley 2008

209. Niezen 2003, pp 14-15

210. Jung 2003

211. Ibid, p 445

212. Ibid, p 459

213. Kingsnorth 2003, pp 28-29

214. Rovira 2000, p 73

215. Hesketh 2013

216. Marcos /Ponce de Lyon 2001, pp 22-23

217. Niezen 2003

218. Ingold 2000

219. Ingold 2003, p 25

220. Hesketh 2013

221. Ibid, p 83

222. Ibid, p 82

223. Hesketh 2013, p 81

224. Ibid, p 77

225. Higgins 2004

226. Marcos/Ponce de Lyon 2001, p 13

227. Riedner 2007

228. Ibid, p 655

229. Ibid, p 643

230. Ibid, p 643

231. Coupe 1997, p 13

232. Di Piramo 2011, p 204

233. Ibid, p 202

234. Di Piramo, p 194

235. Riedner 2007, p 647

236. Ibid, p 647

237. The Kino-nda-niimi Collective 2014, p 21

238. Idle No More 2013

239. Gideon 2006, p 63

240. eg. Larsen 2006, p 317

241. McMahon 2014, p 100

242. Wilson 2014, pp 107-108

243. McLeod 2014, p 128

244. The Kino-nda-niimi Collective 2014

245. Idle No More 2013

246. eg. The Guardian 2011

247. Idle No More 2013

248. Wilson 2013

249. Tully 2000, quoted in Wilson 2013

250. eg. Ingold 2000, Sahlins 2008

251. Coulthard 2010, p 79

252. Larsen 2006, p 314

253. Morgensen 2011

254. Nanibush 2014, p 342

255. Shaw, Herman and Dobbs 2006, p 271

256. Mingolo 2012. Fanon 2001 [1963]

257. Shaw, Herman and Dobbs 2006, p 273

258. Genosko 2009, p 124

259. Maldonado-Torres 2011, p 5

260. Genosko 2009, p 111

261. Deleuze and Guattari 2013 [1980], pp 129-172 and p 130

262. The Ogimaa Mikana Collective 2014, p 332

263. Belcourt 2014, pp 165-166

264. Ibid, p 163

265. McKinver 2014, p 183

266. eg. Larsen 2006. Smith 2001a, pp 111-112

267. eg. Niezen 2003, pp 65-69

268. DruOja Jay 2014, pp 108-112

269. Ibid, p 111

270. Bodley 2008

271. eg. Patrick 2011

272. eg. Jackson 2011

273. eg. Leeuw, et al 2012

274. Gone 2013, p 689

275. Adams 1995, quoted in Gone 2013, p 689

276. eg. Kino-nda-niimi Collective 2014

277. Hunt 2014, p 193

278. Wilson 2014, p 108

279. Gone 2013. Gone 2007. Kirmayer, Gone and Moses 2014. Lester 2013. Nelson 2012

280. McIsaac 2006

281. Gone 2009, quoted in Nelson 2012, p 11

282. Nelson 2012, p 7

283. Gone 2013

284. Wilson 2003

285. Ibid

286. Ibid, p 88

287. Kingsnorth and Hine 2009, p 2 and 7

288. Ibid, p 17

289. Ibid, p 9

290. Ibid, p 2

291. Ibid, p 4

292. Ibid, p 2

293. Ibid, p 3

294. Ibid, p 11-12

295. Ibid, p 13

296. Ibid, p 17

297. Ibid, p 16

298. Ibid, p 15

299. Ibid, p 16

300. eg. Gray 2009

301. The Guardian 2009

302. Ibid

303. Hine 2012

304. McIntosh 2004. McIntosh 2008

305. Kingsnorth and Hine 2009, p 9

306. The Invisible Committee 2009 [2007], p 23

307. Toscano 2009

308. Ibid, p 3

309. The Invisible Committee 2009, pp 52-62

310. Ibid, p 112

311. Kingsnorth and Hine 2009, p 30

312. Ellul 1964 [1954], See also Kidner 2012a, pp. 244-245

313. Fisher 2002, p 172

314. Marcuse 1998 [1941], p. 44

315. Deleuze and Guattari 2013 [1980], pp 420-423

316. Boal 1995, p 169

317. Sale 1996

318. Ibid, p 4

319. Ibid, p.4

320. Ellul 1964 [1954]

321. Giddens 1990

322. Brody 2001, p 97

323. Kidner 2012a, p 240

324. Hardt 1998a, 1998b

325. Ibid, p 140

326. Ibid, p 139

327. Ibid, p 140

328. McIntosh 2004

329. Marcos/de Lyon 2001 [1999], p 213

330. Hardt 1998a, p 140

331. Kingsnorth and Hine 2009, p 31

332. McKenzie 2013

333. eg. Dirzo, R. , Young, H. et al. 2014

334. Yusoff 2012, p 589

335. Blomley 2003

336. Yusoff 2012, p 579

337. Cameron 2012, p 586

338. Kingsnorth and Hine 2014, p 17

339. Gray 2009

340. Cameron 2012

341. Griffin 1982, p 161
342. Deleuze and Guattari 2009 [1972], pp 2-3
343. Ibid, p 5
344. Zerzan 2002, p158
345. Lumsden 2013, p 27
346. Ibid, p 42
347. Bauman 2000
348. Deleuze 1992
349. Berger 2011
350. Deleuze 1992, p 4
351. Ibid, p 7
352. Ibid, p 6
353. Michel 2011, p 174
354. Adorno and Horkheimer 1997 [1944], p 16
355. Coupe 1997, p 13
356. Michel 2011, p 178
357. Vazquez 2012, p 1
358. Ibid, p 3
359. Habermas1989 [1981])
360. Mignolo 2012
361. Maldonato-Torres 2011
362. De Sousa Santos, Nunes, and Meneses 2008
363. Maldonato-Torres 2011, p 2
364. Ibid, p 7
365. Ibid, p 7
366. Kawash 1999, p 242
367. Benjamin quoted in Kawash 1999, p 240
368. Kawash 1999, p 240
369. Smith 2001b, p 32
370. Ibid, p 31
371. Le Corbusier quoted in Smith 2001b, p 31
372. Kidner 2007, p 128
373. Kidner 2007. Kidner 2012a

374. Kidner 2007 p 135

375. eg. Mills 2014

376. Zerzan 2012, pp 1-23 and pp 97-99

377. Ellul quoted in Zerzan 2012, p 98

378. Badiou 2005 [1999], pp 30-31

379. Totton 2011, p 184

380. Postle 2012

381. Genosko 2009, p 124

382. Ibid, p 115

383. Glendinning 2007 [1994]

384. Ibid, p xiii

385. Ibid, pp 90-91

386. Ibid, p 91

387. Ibid, p 93

388. Ibid, pp 97-111

389. Virilio 2007 [2005] p 11

390. Ibid, p 33

391. Bakan 2004, p 55

392. Ibid, p 56

393. Ibid, p 57

394. Alvarez 2014, P ix

395. Ibid, p ix

396. Guattari 2008 [1989], p 28

397. The Invisible Committee 2009 [2007], pp 74-75

398. Mithen 2004, p 95

399. The Invisible Committee 2009 [2007], p 75

400. Mithen 2004, p 95

401. Marcuse 2002 [1964], p 248

402. Guattari 2008 [1989], p 37

403. Guattari 1995 [1992], p 13

404. Ingold 2000, p 316

405. Ibid, p 315

406. Ibid, p 314

407. Ibid, p 316
408. Ibid, p 316
409. Griffin 1982, p 161
410. Bailey 1998. Sale 1996
411. Jones 2006, p 7
412. Ibid, p 6
413. Sale 1996
414. eg. Jones 2006
415. Lewis and Aislin 2015
416. Earth First Journal 2015

BIBLIOGRAPHY

Adorno, T.W. and Horkheimer, M. (1997) [1944]. *Dialectic of Enlightenment*. (London; Verso).

Alexander, J.C. (2013). *The Dark Side of Modernity*. (Cambridge; Polity Press).

Alvarez, N. (2014). *Liminal; a novella*. (Pennsylvania; Black and Green Press).

American Psychiatric Association (APA). (2013). *Diagnostic and Statistical Manual of Mental Disorders, Fifth Edition (DSM-5)*. (Arlington; VA; APA Publishing)

Anderson, B. and Harrison, P. (2010). *Taking-Place: Non-Representational Theories and Geography*. (Farnham; Ashgate).

Anderson, K. (1997). *"A Walk on the Wild Side: A Critical Geography of Domestication"* Progress in Human Geography. 21:4, 463-85.

Anderson, K. and Smith, S. (2001). *"Editorial: Emotional Geographies"* Transactions of the Institute of British Geographers. 26:1, 7-10.

Auge, M. (2009) [1995]. *Non-Places: Introduction to an Anthropology of Supermodernity*. (London; Verso).

Badiou, A. (2005) [1999]. *Philosophy and Desire*. In Badiou, A. (2005) *Infinite Thought*. (London; Continuum) pp 29-42.

Bakan, J. (2004). *The Corporation*. (London; Constable and Robinson Ltd).

Bailey, B. (1998). *The Luddite Rebellion*. (Stroud; Sutton Publishing).

Bauman, Z. (2008). *Does Ethics Have a Chance in a World of Consumers?* (Cambridge, MA: Harvard University Press).

Bauman, Z. (2000). *Liquid Modernity*. (Cambridge; Polity Press).

Becker, M. (2010). *"The Dialectic of Civilization"* unpublished paper, California State University, Fresno. Accessed online 20th March 2014. http://wpsa.research.pdx.edu/meet/2012/beckermichae l.pdf

Belcourt, C. (2014). *Reclaiming Ourselves One Name at a Time*. In ed The Kino-nda-niimi Collective (2014). *The Winter We Danced: Voices from the past, the future and the Idle No More movement*. (Winnipeg, Manitoba; ARP Books).

Bennett, J. (2005). *The Agency of Assemblages and the North American Blackout*. Public Culture. 17:3, 445-465.

Berger, J. (2011). *"Fellow Prisoners"* Guernica Magazine July 2011. www.guernicamag.com/features/ 2875/john_berger_7_15_11/ ; Accessed on 30th July 2011.

Besley, A. C. (2013). *Foucault: The Culture of Self, Subjectivity and Truth-telling Practices*. In eds Dillet,

Blomley, N. (2003). *"Law, Property, and the Geography of Violence: The Frontier, the Survey, and the Grid"* Annals of the Association of American Geographers. 93:1, 121-141.

Boal, I. (1995). *Up From The Bottom*. In ed Katzenberger, E. (1995). *First World, Ha Ha Ha! The Zapatista Challenge*. (San Francisco CA; City Lights

Books).

Bodley, J. (2008). *Victims of Progress*. 5th edition. (Lanham MD; Alta Mira Press).

Bracken P., Thomas P., Timimi S., Asen E., Behr G., Beuster C., Bhunnoo S., Browne I., et al. (2012). "*Psychiatry beyond the current paradigm*" British Journal of Psychiatry, *201*:6, 430-434.

Bracken, P. and Thomas, P. (2005). *Postpsychiatry: mental health in a postmodern world*. (Oxford; Oxford University Press).

Brand, U. and Hirsch, J. (2004). "*In Search of Emancipatory Politics: The Resonances of Zapatism in Western Europe*" Antipode. 36:3, 371-382

Brody, H. (2001). *The Other Side of Eden: Hunter-gatherers, Farmers and the Shaping of the World*. (London; Faber and Faber).

Brown, S. D. and Tucker, I. (2010). *Eff the Ineffable: Affect, Somatic Management, and Mental Health Service Users*, In Gregg, M. and Seigworth, G. J. (2010). *The Affect Theory Reader*. (Durham NC: Duke University Press). pp 229-249.

Buchanan, I. (2008). *Deleuze and Guattari's Anti-Oedipus: a reader's guide*. (London; Continuum).

Buchanan-Barker, P. and Barker, P. (2009). "*The Convenient Myth of Thomas Szasz*" Journal of Psychiatric and Mental Health Nursing.16, 87-95.

Cameron, E. (2012). "*New Geographies of Story and Storytelling*" Progress in Human Geography. 36:5, 573-592.

Carrigan, A. (2001). *Chiapas, The First Postmodern Revolution*. In Marcos, Subcomandante and ed Ponce de Lyon, J. (2001). *Our Word is Our Weapon: Selected Writings of Subcomandante Insurgente Marcos*.

(London; Serpents Tail).

Castree, N. (2005).*Nature*. (London; Routledge).

Clarke, L. (2003). *The Care and Confinement of the Mentally Ill*. In ed Barker, P. (2003). *Psychiatric and Mental Health Nursing: The Craft of Caring*. (London; Arnold) pp 10-18.

Conant, J. (2010). *A Poetics of Resistance: The Revolutionary Public Relations of the Zapatista Insurgency*. (Edinburgh; AK Press).

Conrad, P. (2007). *The medicalization of society: on the transformation of human conditions into treatable disorders*. (Baltimore: Johns Hopkins University Press).

Coppock, V. and Hopton, J. (2001). *Critical perspectives on mental health*. (London; Routledge).

Coulthard, G. (2010). *"Place Against Empire: Understanding Indigenous Anti-Colonialism"* Affinities: A Journal of Radical Theory, Culture, and Action. 4:2, 79-83.

Coupe, L. (1997). *Myth*. (London; Routledge).

Crossley, N. (2006). *Contesting Psychiatry: Social Movements in Mental Health*. (Abingdon; Routledge).

Crossley, N. (1998). *"R. D. Laing and the British Anti-Psychiatry Movement: A Socio-Historical Analysis"* Social Science and Medicine 57:7, 877-889.

Davies, A., Hoggart, K., and Lees, L. (2001). *Researching Human Geography*. (London: Hodder Education).

Debord, G. [1955]. *Introduction to a Critique of Urban Geography*. Accessed on 5th December 2013 via the Situationist International Archive: http://www.cddc. vt.edu/sionline/presitu/geography.html

Delanty, G. (1999). *Social Theory in a Changing*

World: Conceptions of Modernity. (Malden, MA: Polity).

Deleuze, G. (1992). *"Postscript on the societies of control"* October Journal. *59*, 3-7.

Deleuze, G. and Guattari, F. (2013) [1980]. *A Thousand Plateaus: Capitalism and Schizophrenia.* (London; Bloomsbury Academic).

Deleuze, G. and Guattari, F. (2009) [1972]. *Anti-Oedipus: Capitalism and Schizophrenia.* (London: Penguin Books).

Diamond, J. (1998). *Guns, Germs and Steel: a short history of everybody for the last 13,000 years.* (London; Vintage).

Dillet B., MacKenzie, I. and Porter, R. (2013). *The Edinburgh Companion to Poststructuralism.* (Edinburgh; Edinburgh University Press).

Dittmer, J. (2014). *"Geopolitical assemblages and complexity"* Progress in human Geography, 2014, 38:3, 385-401.

Di Piramo, D. (2011). *"Beyond Modernity: Irony, Fantasy and the Challenge to Grand Narratives in Subcomandante Marcos' Tales"* Mexican Studies/Estudios Mexicanos, 27:1, 177-205.

Dirzo, R., Young, H., Galetti, M., Ceballos,G., Isaac, N., and Collen, B. (2014). *"Defaunation in the Anthropocene"* Science, 345:6195, 401-406.

DruOja Jay. (2014). *What if Natives stop subsidizing Canada?* In ed The Kino-nda-niimi Collective. (2014). *The Winter We Danced: Voices from the past, the future and the Idle No More movement.* (Winnipeg, Manitoba; ARP Books)pp 108-111.

Earth First Journal. (2015). *"Coal Derailment in Solidarity with Imprisoned Anarchists".* Accessed

online 23rd June 2015: http://earthfirstjournal.org/
newswire/2015/06/15/coal-derailment-in-solidarity-
with-imprisoned-anarchists/

Ellul, J. (1964) [1954]. *The Technological Society*.
(Toronto: Vintage Books).

Fanon, F. (2001) [1963]. *The Wretched of the Earth*.
(London; Penguin).

Fisher, A. (2002). *Radical Ecopsychology: psychology
in the service of life*. (Albany, NY: State University of
New York Press).

Foucault, M. (1991) [1975]. *Discipline and Punish:
The birth of the prison*. (London; Penguin).

Foucault, M. (2002) [1969]. *The Archaeology of
Knowledge*. (London; Routledge).

Fox, N. J. (1995). *Postmodernism, Sociology and
Health*. (Buckingham; Open University Press).

Freud, S. (2004) [1930]. *Civilisation and its
Discontents*. (London; Penguin).

Genosko, G. (2009). *Felix Guattari: A Critical
Introduction*. (London; Pluto Press).

Genosko, G. (ed). (1996). *The Guattari Reader*.
(Oxford; Blackwell).

Gideon, V. (2006) *Canadian Aboriginal peoples tackle
e-health*. In ed Landzelius, K (2006). *Native on the
Net: Indigenous and Diasporic Peoples in the Virtual
Age*. (Abingdon; Routledge). pp 61-79.

Giddens, A. (1991). *Modernity and self-identity: Self
and society in the late modern age*. (Cambridge;
Polity).

Giddens, A. (1990). *The Consequences of Modernity*.
(Oxford; Blackwell).

Glendinning, C. (2007) [1994]. *My Name is Chellis
and I'm in recovery from Western Civilization*.

(Gabriola Island BC; New Catalyst Books).

Gone, J. (2013). *"Redressing First Nations historical trauma: Theorizing mechanisms for indigenous culture as mental health treatment"* Transcultural Psychiatry, 50:5, 683-706.

Gone, J. (2007). *"We Never was Happy Living Like a Whiteman" Mental Health Disparities and the Postcolonial Predicament in American Indian Communities"* American Journal of Community Psychology, 2007, 40, 290-300.

Gonzalez, X. O. (2010). *"Deny Anarchic Spaces and Places: An Anarchist Critique of Mosaic-Statist Metageography"* Anarchist Developments in Cultural Studies, 2010 (1). Accessed online 20th October 2013: http://theanarchistlibrary.org/library/xavier-oliveras-gonzalez-deny-anarchic-spaces-and-places-an-anarchist-critique-of-mosaic-statist

Gray, J. (2009). *"Walking on Lava"* New Statesman, 14th September 2009, pp42-43.

Griffin, S. (1982). *The Way of All Ideology.* pp 161-181 in Griffin, S. *Made from this Earth; Selections from her writing.* (London; Women's Press Ltd).

Griffin, S. (1994) [1978]. *Woman and Nature: the roaring inside her.* (London: The Women's Press Ltd).

Griffiths, J. (2000). *Pip Pip: a sideways look at time.* (London: Flamingo)

The Guardian (2011). *"The Truth about Twitter, Facebook and the uprisings in the Arab world"*, 25th February 2011. Accessed online 16 April 2015: http://www.theguardian.com/world/2011/feb/25/twitter-facebook-uprisings-arab-libya

The Guardian (2009), Kingsnorth, P and Monbiot, G. *"Is there any point in fighting to stave off industrial apocalypse?"* 18th August 2009, print edition, p 30.

Guattari, F. (2013) [1989]. *Schizoanalytic Cartographies*. (London; Bloomsbury Academic).

Guattari, F. (2011) [1979]. *The Machinic Unconscious: Essays in Schizoanalysis*. (Los Angeles, CA: Semiotext(e)).

Guattari, F. (2009a). *Chaosophy: Texts and Interviews 1972-1977*. (Los Angeles, CA: Semiotext(e)).

Guattari, F. (2009b). *Soft Subversions: Texts and Interviews 1977-1985*. (Los Angeles, CA: Semiotext(e)).

Guattari, F. (2008) [1989]. *The Three Ecologies*. (London: Continuum).

Guattari, F. (1995) [1992]. *Chaosmosis: an ethico-aesthetic paradigm*. (Sydney: Power Publications).

Habermas, J. (1989) [1981]. *The Theory of Communicative Action, Volume Two: The Critique of Functionalist Reason*. (Cambridge; Polity Press).

Hansen, J. (2011). *Storms of my Grandchildren*. (New York: Bloomsbury).

Hardt, M. (1998a). *"The global society of control" Discourse, 20*:3, 139-152.

Hardt, M. (1998b). *The Withering of Civil Society*. In eds Kaufman, E. and Heller, K. J. (1998). *Deleuze and Guattari; new mappings in politics, philosophy and culture*. (Minneapolis MN; University of Minnesota Press) pp 23-39.

Henck, N. (2007). *Subcommander Marcos: The Man and the Mask*. (Durham NC; Duke University Press).

Hesketh, C. (2013). *"The Clash of Spatializations: Geopolitics and Class Struggles in Southern Mexico"* Latin American Perspectives. Issue 191, 40:4, 70-87.

Hidaka, B. H. (2012). *"Depression as a disease of*

modernity: explanations for increasing prevalence" Journal of Affective Disorder, 140:3, 205-214.

Higgins, N. P. (2004). *Understanding the Chiapas Rebellion: Modernist Visions and the Invisible Indian.* (Austin TX; University of Texas Press).

Hine, D. (2012). *"A Question of Billing"* Dark Mountain Project Blog 31st October 2012. Accessed 10th February 2015. http://dark-mountain.net/blog/a-question-of-billing/

Holbrook-Pierson, M. (2006). *The Place You Love is Gone: progress hits home.* (New York; W. W. Norton & Co).

Holland, E. W. (2013). *Deleuze and Guattari's A Thousand Plateaus.* (London; Bloomsbury Academic).

Holland, E. W. (1999). *Deleuze and Guattari's Anti-Oedipus: Introduction to Schizoanalysis.* (London; Routledge).

Holloway, J. (1998). *Dignity's Revolt.* In eds Holloway and Pelaez. (1998). *Zapatista! Reinventing Revolution in Mexico.* (London; Pluto Press).

Holmes, D., Gastaldo, D., & Perron, A. (2007). *"Paranoid investments in nursing: A schizoanalysis of the evidence-based discourse"* Nursing Philosophy, 8:2, 85-91.

Holmes, D., Murray, S., Perron, A. and Rail, G. (2006). *"Deconstructing the evidence-based discourse in health sciences: truth, power and fascism"* International Journal of Evidence Based Healthcare. 2006, 4: 180-186.

Hopton, J. (1997). *"Towards a Critical Theory of Mental Health Nursing"* Journal of Advanced Nursing.25, 492-500.

Horkheimer, M. (2012) [1974]. *Critique of*

Instrumental Reason. (London; Verso).

Idle No More (2013). *The Manifesto.* Accessed online on 13th June 2014: www.idlenomore.ca/manifesto

Illich, I. (1977) [1975]. *Limits to Medicine. Medical Nemesis: The Expropriation of Health.* (London: Pelican).

Ince, A. (2012). *"In The Shell of the Old: Anarchist Geographies of Territorialisation"* Antipode, 44:5, pp 1645-1666

Ingold, T. (2000). *The Perception of the Environment: Essays in livelihood, dwelling and skill.* (London; Routledge).

The Invisible Committee (2009) [2007]. *The Coming Insurrection.* (Los Angeles, CA: Semiotext(e))

Jackson, D. (2011). *"Scents of place: the dysplacement of a First Nations community in Canada"* American Anthropologist, 113:4, 606-18.

Johnstone, L. (2008). *Psychiatric Diagnosis.* In eds Tummey, R. and Turner, T. (2008). *Critical Issues in Mental Health.* (Basingstoke; Palgrave Macmillan).

Jones, S E. (2006). *Against Technology: From the Luddites to Neo-Luddism.* (Abingdon; Routledge).

Jung, C. (2003). *"The Politics of Indigenous Identity: Neoliberalism, Cultural Rights and the Mexican Zapatistas"* Social Research, 70:2, 433-462.

Karim H. K. (2001). *"Cyber-Utopia and the Myth of Paradise: using Jacques Ellul's work on propaganda to analyse information society rhetoric"* Information, Communication and Society, 4:1, 113-134.

Kawash, S. (1999). *Terrorists and Vampires: Fanon's Spectral Violence of Decolonization.* In ed Alessandrini, A. (1999). *Frantz Fanon: Critical Perspectives.* (London; Routledge) pp 235-257.

Kidner, D. (2012a). *Nature and Experience in the Culture of Delusion: How Industrial Society Lost Touch with Reality.* (Basingstoke; Palgrave Macmillan).

Kidner, D. (2012b). *"Exploring the Farther Reaches of Commoditization: A Systemic Perspective"* Bulletin of Science, Technology and Society. 32:1, 18-30.

Kidner, D. (2007). *"Depression and the Natural World: Towards a Critical Ecology of Psychological Distress"* Critical Psychology. 19, 123-146.

Kingsnorth, P. and Hine, D. (2014). *Uncivilisation: The Dark Mountain Manifesto.* (Self-published 2nd edition: The Dark Mountain Project).

Kingsnorth, P. and Hine, D. (2009). *Uncivilisation: The Dark Mountain Manifesto.* (Rochdale; Bracketpress).

Kingsnorth, P. (2003). *One No, Many Yesses: A Journey to the Heart of the Global Resistance Movement.* (London; The Free Press).

The Kino-nda-niimi Collective eds (2014). *The Winter We Danced: Voices from the past, the future and the Idle No More movement.* (Winnipeg, Manitoba; ARP Books).

Kirmayer, L., Gone, J. and Moses, J. (2014). *"Rethinking Historical Trauma"* Transcultural Psychiatry, 51:3, 299-319.

Klein, N. (2000). *No logo: No space, no choice, no jobs.* (London: Flamingo).

Koopman, C. (2013). *Genealogy as Critique: Foucault and the problems of modernity.* (Bloomington: Indiana University Press).

Larsen, S. C. (2006). *"The Future's Past: Politics of time and territory among Dakelh first nations in*

British Colombia" Geografiska Annaler. Series B, Human Geography, 88:3, 311-321.

Leboyer, F. (1987) [1974]. *Birth Without Violence.* (London; Fontana/Collins).

Leeuw, S., Maurice, S., Holyk, T., Greenwood, M and Adam, W. (2012). *"With Reserves: Colonial Geographies and First Nations Health"* Annals of the Association of American Geographers, 2012, 102:5, 904-911.

Lefebvre, H. (1991). *The Production of Space.* (Oxford; Blackwell).

Lester, R. (2013). *"Back from the edge of existence: A critical anthropology of trauma"* Transcultural Psychiatry, 50:3 753-762.

Levi-Strauss, C. (2013) [1978]. *Myth and Meaning.* (London: Routledge).

Lewis, B. (2006). *Moving beyond Prozac, DSM, & the new psychiatry: the birth of postpsychiatry.* (Ann Arbor: University of Michigan Press).

Lewis, S.L. and Maslin, M.A. (2015). *"Defining the Anthropocene"* Nature, 2015 Mar 12;519:7542, 171-80

Lovelock, J. (2006).*The Revenge of Gaia.* (London: Allen Lane).

Lucas R.H. and Barrett R.J. (1995). *"Interpreting Culture and Psychopathology: primitivist themes in cross-cultural debate"* Culture, Medicine and Psychiatry 19:3, 287-326.

Lumsden, S. (2013). *Poststructuralism and Modern European Philosophy.* In eds Dillet, B., MacKenzie, I. and Porter, R. (2013). *The Edinburgh Companion to Poststructuralism.* (Edinburgh University Press.)pp 23-46

Lyotard, J. F. (1984). *The postmodern condition: A*

report on knowledge. (Manchester: Manchester University Press).

Maldonado-Torres, N. (2011). *"Thinking through the Decolonial Turn: Post-continental Interventions in Theory, Philosophy and Critique – An Introduction"* Transmodernity. Fall 2011. pp. 1-15.

Marcos, Subcomandante. (2007). *Beyond Resistance: Everything: an interview.* (Durham NC; Paper Boat Press).

Marcos, Subcomandante. (2006). *The Other Campaign; La Otra Campana.* (San Francisco; City Lights Books).

Marcos, Subcommandante. (2003) [1996]. *The Story of the Colours/La Historia De Los Colores.* (El Paso, TX; Cinco Puntos Press)

Marcos, Subcomandante and Ignacio Taibo II, P. (2007) [2005]. *The Uncomfortable Dead.* (London; Serpents Tail).

Marcos, Subcomandante and Ponce de Lyon, J. (2001). *Our Word is Our Weapon: Selected Writings of Subcomandante Insurgente Marcos.* (London; Serpents Tail).

Marcuse, H. (2002) [1964]. *One-Dimensional Man.* (Abingdon; Routledge).

Marcuse, H. (1998) [1941]. *Some Social Implications of Modern Technology.* In Technology, War and Fascism: Collected Papers of Herbert Marcuse Vol 1. (London; Routledge) pp 39-65.

McIntosh, A. (2008). *Hell and High Water: Climate change, hope and the human condition.* (Edinburgh; Birlinn Limited).

McIntosh, A. (2004). *Soil and Soul: People Versus Corporate Power.* (London; Aurum Press).

McIsaac, M. (2006). *"A First Nations perspective on mental health in the North"* BC Medical Journal, May 2006, 48:4, 178-179.

McKenzie, B. (2013). *"Good Grief"* Dark Mountain Project Blog, 26th November 2013. accessed 20th February 2015. http://dark-mountain.net/blog/good-grief/

McKinver, M. (2014). *How do you say Idle No More in Anishinaabemowin?* In eds The Kino-nda-niimi Collective. (2014). *The Winter We Danced: Voices from the past, the future and the Idle No More movement.* (Winnipeg, Manitoba; ARP Books) pp 182-183.

McLeod, N. (2014). *Nothing Will Ever Be The Same: Idle No More.* In eds The Kino-nda-niimi Collective. (2014). *The Winter We Danced: Voices from the past, the future and the Idle No More movement.* (Winnipeg, Manitoba; ARP Books) pp 127-129

McLuhan, M, (2003) [1964]. *Understanding media: The extensions of man.* (London; Routledge).

McMahon, R. (2014). *The Round Dance Revolution.* pp 98-102. In eds The Kino-nda-niimi Collective. (2014). *The Winter We Danced: Voices from the past, the future and the Idle No More movement.* (Winnipeg, Manitoba; ARP Books) pp 98-102

Michel, A. (2011). *"Psychiatry after Virtue: a modern practice in the ruins"* Journal of Medicine and Philosophy. 36:2, 170-186

Midgley, M. (2003). *The Myths We Live By.* (London: Routledge).

Mignolo, W. (2012). *The Darker Side of Western Modernity: Global Futures, Decolonial Options.* (Durham, NC; Duke University Press).

Mills, C. (2014). *Decolonizing Global Mental Health:*

The psychiatrization of the majority world. (Hove; Routledge).

Mithen, S. (2004). *After the Ice: a global human history 20,000-5000 BC.* (London; Orion Books).

Monbiot, G. (2007). *Heat: how we can stop the planet burning.* (London: Penguin).

Morgensen, S. L. (2011) *"The Biopolitics of Settler Colonialism: Right Here, Right Now"* Settler Colonial Studies, 1:1, 52-76

Mumford, L. (2010) [1934]. *Technics and Civilization.* (Chicago Il: University of Chicago Press).

Nail, T. (2012). *Returning to Revolution: Deleuze, Guattari and Zapatismo.* (Edinburgh University Press).

Nail, T. (2010). *"A Post-Neoliberal Ecopolitics? Deleuze, Guattari and Zapatismo"* Philosophy Today, Summer 2010.

Nanibush, W. (2014). *Idle No More: Strong Hearts of Women's Leadership.* In eds The Kino-nda-niimi Collective. (2014). *The Winter We Danced: Voices from the past, the future and the Idle No More movement.* (Winnipeg, Manitoba; ARP Books) pp 341-344

Nelson, S. (2012). *Challenging Hidden Assumptions: Colonial Norms as Determinants of Aboriginal Mental Health.* (Prince George BC; National Collaborating Centre for Aboriginal Health, University of Northern British Columbia).

Niezen, R. (2003). *The Origins of Indigenism: human rights and the politics of identity.* (Berkeley CA; University of California Press)

Oakley, A. (1980). *Woman Confined: Towards a Sociology of Childbirth.* (Oxford: Martin Robertson and Co).

The Ogimaa Mikana Collective. (2014). *The Ogimaa Mikana Project*. In eds The Kino-nda-niimi Collective. (2014). *The Winter We Danced: Voices from the past, the future and the Idle No More movement*. (Winnipeg, Manitoba; ARP Books). pp 329-332.

Patrick, R. (2011). *"Uneven access to safe drinking water for First Nations in Canada: connecting health and place through source water protection"* Health and Place. 17:1, 386-9.

Peacock, J. W. and Nolan, P. W. (2000). *"Care under threat in the modern world"*, Journal of Advanced Nursing. 2000, 32:5, 1066-1070.

Pilgrim, D. (2007). *"The survival of psychiatric diagnosis"*, Social Science & Medicine, *65*:3, 536-547.

Pink, S. (2012). *Situating Everyday Life*. (London; Sage).

Polack, J-C. (2011). *Analysis, between Psycho and Schizo*. In eds Goffey, A and Alliez, E. (2011). *The Guattari Effect*. (London: Continuum). pp 57-67.

Postle, D. (2012). *Therapy Futures; Obstacles and Opportunities*. (Wentworth Learning Resources).

Rabinow, P. (1991) [1984]. *The Foucault Reader: An Introduction to Foucault's Thought*. (London; Penguin).

Riedner, R. (2007). *"Affective Encounters: Writing Zapatismo"* JAC, 27:3/4, 637-664

Roberts, M. (2007). *"Capitalism, Psychiatry, and Schizophrenia: a critical introduction to Deleuze and Guattari's Anti-Oedipus"* Nursing Philosophy. 8, 114-127.

Ronfeldt, D. (1998). *The Zapatista Social Netwar in Mexico*. (Santa Monica, CA; RAND)

Rovira, G. (2000). *Women of Maize: Indigenous*

Women and the Zapatista Rebellion. (London; Latin America Bureau).

Sadler, J.Z. (2005).*Values and Psychiatric Diagnosis.* (Oxford; Oxford University Press).

Sahlins, M. (2008). The Western Illusion of Human Nature. (Chicago IL; Prickly Paradigm Press).

Sale, K. (1995). *Rebels Against The Future: The Luddites and their war on the Industrial Revolution.* (Reading MA; Addison-Wesley Publishing Company).

Santos, B. de Sousa, Nunes, J A, and Meneses, M P. (2008). *Introduction: Opening up the Canon of Knowledge and Recognition of Difference.* In ed Santos, B. de Sousa (2008). *Another Knowledge is Possible: Beyond Northern Epistemologies.* (London; Verso) pp. xviii-lxii.

Sauvagnargues, A. (2011). *A Schizoanalytic Knight on the Chessboard of Politics.* In eds Goffey, A. and Alliez, E. (2011). *The Guattari Effect.* (London: Continuum) pp 172-185

Shaw, W. S., Herman, R.D.K. and Dobbs, G. R. (2006), *"Encountering Indigeneity: Re-imagining and decolonizing geography"* Geografiska Annaler: Series B, Human Geography, 88, 267–276.

Silverman, D. (2013). *Doing Qualitative Research.* (London: SAGE Publications Ltd).

Simonsen, K. (2007). *"Practice, Spatiality and Embodied Emotions: An outline of a Geography of Practice"* Human Affairs. 17, 168-181.

Smith, L. T. (1999). *Decolonizing Methodologies: Research and Indigenous Peoples.* (London; Zed Books).

Smith, M. (2007). *"Wild-life: Anarchy, Ecology, and Ethics"* Environmental Politics. 16:3, 470-87.

Smith, M. (2001a). *An Ethics of Place*. (Albany, NY: State University of New York Press).

Smith, M. (2001b). *"Repetition and Difference: Lefebvre, Le Corbusier and Modernity's (Im)moral Landscape"* Ethics, Place and Environment. 4:1, 31-44.

Springer, S. 2014b. *"For anarcho-geography! Or, bare-knuckle boxing as the world burns"* Dialogues in Human Geography. 4:3, 297–310.

Springer, S. (2014a). *"Why a radical geography must be anarchist"* Dialogues in Human Geography. 4:3, 249–270.

Stiglitz, J. (2003). *Globalization and Its Discontents*. (London: Penguin).

Szasz, T. S. (2009). *Antipsychiatry: quackery squared*. (Syracuse, N.Y.: Syracuse University Press).

Szasz, T. S. (1974).*Law, liberty and psychiatry: An inquiry into the social uses of mental health practices*. (London: Routledge and Kegan Paul).

Thrift, N. J. (2007). *Non-representational theory: Space, politics, affect*. (Abingdon, Oxon; Routledge).

Tormey, S. (2006). *"'Not in my Name': Deleuze, Zapatismo and the Critique of Representation"* Parliamentary Affairs, 59:1, 138-154.

Toscano (2009). *"The war against pre-terrorism: The Tarnac 9 and The Coming Insurrection"* Radical philosophy 154, Mar/Apr 2009.

Totton, N. (2011) *Wild Therapy: undomesticating inner and outer worlds*. (Ross-on-Wye; PCCS Books)

Vaneigem, R. (2012) [1967]. *The Revolution of Everyday Life*. (Oakland, CA; PM Press).

Vazquez, R. (2012). *"Towards a Decolonial Critique of Modernity BuenVivir, Relationality and the Task of*

Listening" Capital, Poverty, Development 2012, 33, 241-252. Accessed online 12th October 2014. http://www.ceapedi.com.ar/imagenes/biblioteca/libros/241.pdf

Vetter, G. (2012). *The Architecture of Control: A Contribution to the Critique of the Science of Apparatuses.* (Lanham: John Hunt Publishing).

Virilio, P. (2008) [1995]. *Open sky.* (London; Verso).

Virilio, P. (2007) [2005]. *The Original Accident.* (Cambridge; Polity Press).

Virilio, P. (2002). *Ground Zero.* (London; Verso).

Whitehill, I. (2003). *The Concept of Recovery.* In ed Barker, P. (2003). *Psychiatric and Mental Health Nursing: The Craft of Caring.* (London; Arnold) pp 43-49.

Williams, S. (2002). *The Nature of Schizophrenia.* In eds Harris, N, Williams, S and Bradshaw, T. (2002). *Psychosocial Interventions for People with Schizophrenia.* (Basingstoke; Palgrave Macmillan)pp 3-17

Wilson, K. (2003). *"Therapeutic landscapes and First Nations peoples: an exploration of culture, health and place"* Health and Place, 2003, 9, 83-93.

Wilson, N. (2014). *KisikewIskwew, The Woman Spirit.* In eds The Kino-nda-niimi Collective. (2014). *The Winter We Danced: Voices from the past, the future and the Idle No More movement.* (Winnipeg, Manitoba; ARP Books) pp 102-108.

Wilson, N. (2013). *Idle No More: An Essay Introducing Treaty, Internal Colonization and Native Nationalism.* Ecopost Blog, 25th September 2013. Accessed on 13th June 2014. https://ecopostblog.wordpress.com/2013/09/25/idle-no-more-an-essay-introducing-treaty-internal-colonization-and-native-nationalism/

WHO: World Health Organisation. (1992). *ICD-10 Classification of Mental and Behavioural Disorders.* (Geneva; WHO).

Yusoff, K. (2012). *"Aesthetics of Loss: biodiversity, banal violence and biotic subjects"* Transactions of the Institute of British Geographers. 2012, 37, 578-592.

Zerzan, J. (2012). *Future Primitive Revisited.* (Los Angeles; Feral House).

Zerzan, J. (2008). *Twilight of the Machines.* (Los Angeles; Feral House).

Zerzan, J. (ed). (2005). *Against Civilization: Readings and Reflections.* (Los Angeles; Feral House).

Also from Winter Oak

Paul Cudenec – *Nature, Essence and Anarchy (2016)*

Paul Cudenec – *The Fakir of Florence: A Novel in Three Layers (2016)*

Paul Cudenec – *Forms of Freedom (2015)*

Paul Cudenec – *The Stifled Soul of Humankind (2104)*

Paul Cudenec – *The Anarchist Revelation: Being What We're Meant to Be (2103)*

Paul Cudenec – *Antibodies, Anarchangels and Other Essays (2013)*

Richard Jefferies – *The Story of My Heart (2015)*

Henry Salt – *Richard Jefferies: His Life and Ideals (2015)*

Full details of all these titles are available on the Winter Oak website at www.winteroak.org.uk, along with our regular anti-capitalist information bulletin The Acorn. To get in touch with Winter Oak please email winteroak@greenmail.net or follow @winteroakpress on Twitter.

ABOUT THE AUTHOR

Ed Lord is an activist, researcher and mental health nurse based in South Wales. Get in touch via modernmadness@riseup.net or on Twitter @modern_madness

Made in the USA
Middletown, DE
15 August 2024

59162023R00126